AF541260

PROBLEMS AND PROSPECTS OF WOMEN ENTREPRENEURSHIP

PROBLEMS AND PROSPECTS OF WOMEN ENTREPRENEURSHIP

Edited by

Dr. Suman Kalyan Chaudhury

M.Com, MBA, PGDPM & IR, LLB, Ph.D.

Reader cum Placement Officer

P.G. Department of Business Administration

Berhampur University

Berhampur

(Odisha)

DISCOVERY PUBLISHING HOUSE PVT. LTD.

NEW DELHI-110 002

Published by:

Tilak Wasan

DISCOVERY PUBLISHING HOUSE PVT. LTD.
4383/4A, Ansari Road, Darya Ganj
New Delhi-110 002 (India)
Phone : +91-11-23279245, 43596064-65
Fax : +91-11-23253475
E-mail : parul.wasan@gmail.com
discoverypublishinghouse@gmail.com
web : www.discoverypublishinggroup.com

***First Edition:* 2012**
ISBN: 978-93-5056-050-1

Problems and Prospects of Women Entrepreneurship

Printed at:
Shree Balaji Art Press
Delhi

Preface

Women entrepreneurship is a very fascinating subject in the present advanced era. The more one reads various texts on this subject, it is more absorbing does it become. Women are almost one & half of the world's population having enormous potential but being underutilized or unutilized for the economic development of the nation. Majority of women do not undertake entrepreneurial ventures. There is a need to strength and streamline the role of women in the development of various sectors by harnessing their power towards nation building and to attain accelerated economic growth process. Alleviation of poverty, the core of all development efforts has remained a very complex and critical concern among developing countries. The World Bank recommended that the surest and the only way to lift India out of poverty is to educate and enhance the status of country's women. Similar observations have been made by Mahatma Gandhi and Pandit Jawaharlal Lal Nehru as well. The Indian sociological set up has been traditionally a male dominate done. Women are considered as weaker sex and always to depend on men-folk in their family and outside, throughout their life. They are left with lesser commitments and kept as a dormant force for a quite long time. The Indian culture made them only subordinates and executors of the decisions made by other male members, in the basic family structure.

Women are the nuclei of a nation. They are the real builder and moulder of a nation's destiny. The position and status of women in any society is an index of its civilization and progress. Though the number of women-owned businesses is booming today, it is argued that many of these women don't have million-dollar businesses because they don't imagine taking their businesses to the next level. While juggling everything in their personal and professional lives, many women fail to grow their businesses because they don't know if everything will get out of hand. Though more than half-a-century has passed after independence, development of women entrepreneurship has not been rapidly achieved as the other measures of development. The question arise that why this scenario exists? Who is responsible for it? What is to be done to overcome the problems of women entrepreneurship? This edited volume relates to all the above questions and provides probable answers to them. This book also tries to make a humble effort to include entrepreneurial attitude and enhancing self-employment among women with the help of innovative ideas and suggestive measures of all authors.

Dr. Suman Kalyan Chaudhury

Acknowledgements

Every action requires an initiator, influencer. I am initiated into writing this book, primarily, by the inspiration provided by my students and friends in the same profession. My colleagues are always stand with for support and cheering me. Therefore, I can't but gratefully acknowledge my indebtedness to all those who have extended generous assistance in the successful accomplishment of this indispensable work. It will be a serious blunder if I forget to mention some of my colleagues Prof.Niranjan Nayak , Center Head, Koustav Business School, Dr.Kirti Ranjan Swain, Associate Prof., IPSAR Business School, Cuttack, Dr. Ashok Kumar Panigrahi, Asst. Prof, RITEE Business School, Raipur, Prof. Ashok Kumar Panda, Dean, Astha School of Management for their ardent encouragement and beacon guidance in bringing out this work.

I profusely thank my Chairman of the institute, Er. Sundhansu Kumar Dash for his rock support and continuous push that furthered my efforts seamlessly towards quick accomplishment. My heartfelt gratitude to him.

Last but not least my heartfelt gratitude to my wife Sinu knows no bounds for her immaculate co-operation. Needless to depict, I am indebted to my family members for their love and affection and inspired me in my problem solving while in action.

I am also much beholden to Mr. Tilak Wasan, Managing Director, Discovery Publishing House Pvt. Ltd., New Delhi for publishing the work in a record time.

Dr. Suman Kalyan Chaudhury

Contents

Contributors

Dr. Ashok Kumar Panigrahi, Associate Professor, Dept. of Commerce and Management, REET School of Management, Raipur, Chhattisgarh.

Dr. Arvinda.S, Professor, Dept. of Management, College of Business and Economics, Adi-Haqi Campus, Mekelle University, P.O.Box:451, Mekelle, Tigray, Ethiopia.

Dr. Jiwan Jhunjhunwale, Lecturer in Commerce, P.G. Dept. of Commerce, Utkal University, Bhubaneswar, Orissa.

Prof. H.D.Barad, Assistance Professor, Head Department of Commerce, Late Shri N.R.Boricha Education Trust Sanchalit, Arts & Commerce College Mendarda-362260.

Prof. A.K.Panda, Dean, Astha School of Business Management, Bhubaneswar, Orissa.

Dr. Sanjay R. Ajmeri, Lecturer in Com. & Mgt, Bhikahbhai Jivabhai Vanijya Mahavidyalaya, Vallabh Vidyanagar, Anand (Gujarat).

Prof. Trilok Nath Shukla, Senior Lecturer, Bharatiya Vidya Bhavan, Bhubaneswar, Orissa.

Prof. Chumuki Chatarjee, Lecturer, Bharatiya Vidya Bhavan, Bhubaneswar, Orissa.

Dr. S.K.Chaudhury, M.Com, MBA, PGDPM & IR, Ph.D., Reader cum Placement Officer, Department of MBA., Berhampur University, Berhampur, (Odisha).

Dr. K.R.Swain, Sr. Faculty, IPSAR B School, Cuttack, Orissa.

Dr. N.Nayak, Center Head, Koustav Business School, Bhubaneswar, Orissa.

Dr. Sushil Kumar Pattanaik, Senior Faculty in the Dept. of Commerce, KBDAV College, Nirakarpur, KHURDA, Odisha.

Dr. S.K.Das, Senior Faculty, Dept of Commerce, PN (auto) College, KHURDA, Orissa.

Dr. Veershetty Tadlapur, Asst. Prof, Dept. of Sociology, Govt. First Grade College, Kalgi-585312, Karnataka.

Dr. Kallinath S Patil, Associate Professor, Dept. of Commerce and Management Govt. College, Gulbarga-585106.

Dr. Pandit C Bilamge, Associate Professor, Dept. of Commerce and Management Govt. College, Gulbarga 585106.

Dr. Santosh Singh Bais, Assistant Professor, Dept. of Commerce and Management Government. First Grade College, Chincholi 585307.

1

Women Entrepreneurship in India
Prospects and Challenges

Dr. Ashok Kumar Panigrahi

ABSTRACT

Women owned businesses are highly increasing in the economies of almost all countries. The hidden entrepreneurial potentials of women have gradually been changing with the growing sensitivity to the role and economic status in the society. Skill, knowledge and adaptability in business are the main reasons for women to emerge into business ventures. 'Women Entrepreneur' is a person who accepts challenging role to meet her personal needs and become economically independent. In India, although women constitute the majority of the total population, the entrepreneurial world is still a male dominated one. Women in advanced nations are recognized and are more prominent in the business world. Keeping these views on entrepreneurship, this article deals with the problems, which these self-motivated Indian women entrepreneurs can front, and then highlights the present status and the future challenges of women entrepreneurship in India and suggestions for its developments.

Key Words Women Entrepreneurship, Indian economy, Business enterprise

INTRODUCTION

When we speak about the term Women Entrepreneurship we mean, an act of business ownership and business creation that empowers women economically, increases their economic strength as well asposition in society. Hence women-entrepreneurs have been making a considerable impact in all most all the segments ofthe economy which is more than 25 per cent of all kinds of business.In India 'Entrepreneurship' is very limited amongst women especially in the formal sector, which is less than 5 per cent of all the business.

Women Entrepreneurs may be defined as the women or a group of women who initiate, organize and operate a business enterprise. Government of India has defined women entrepreneurs as an enterprise owned and controlled by a women having a minimum financial interest of 51 per cent of the capital and giving at least 51 per cent of employment generated in the enterprise to women. Like a male entrepreneurs a women entrepreneur has many functions. They should explore the prospects of starting new enterprise; undertake risks, introduction of new innovations, coordination administration and control of business and providing effective leadership in all aspects of business.

Women in business are a recent phenomenon in India. By and large they had confide themselves to petty business and tiny cottage industries. Women entrepreneurs engaged in business due to push and pull factors, which encourage women to have an independent occupation and stands on their own legs. A sense towards independent decision-making on their life and career is the motivational factor behind this urge. Saddled with household chores and domestic responsibilities women want to get independence under the influence of these factors the women entrepreneurs choose a profession as a challenge and as an urge to do something new. Such situation is described as pull factors. While in push factors women engaged in business activities due to family compulsion and the responsibility is thrust upon them.

GLOBAL TREND OF WOMEN ENTREPRENEURSHIP

In his paper titled ***"An Insight into the emergence of women-owned businesses as an economic force in india"***, Prof. Surinder Pal Singh has studied the trend of women entrepreneurship all over the world. He found that, although information about women entrepreneurs keeps proliferating, comparatively little is known about women business owners, particularly in developing countries. Research has shown that women-owned firms comprise between one-quarter and one-third of all the businesses in the formal economy and are expected to play an even larger role in informal sectors.

In various studies of entrepreneurial behaviour, women have expressed optimism about the future of their businesses and about their role in the economy. In the words of a Polish Business Owner "I have full control of my business. I approach every problem differently and it is challenging. You have a feeling that you are creating this country."

A study conducted by NFWBO has highlighted that the most important issues cited by women business owners around the world included maintaining profitability, managing cash flow & bill payment, attracting and keeping quality employees, access to latest technology, access to capital for business growth, and government corruption. Even though women entrepreneurs all around the world share these similar reasons for starting their businesses, there are some stark differences for women in other countries that are worth noting.

In India, womens' entry into business is a new phenomenon. It can be traced out as an extension of their kitchen activities mainly to 3Ps viz. Pickles, Powder and Pappad. But with growing awareness about business and spread of education among women over the period, they have started shifting from 3Ps to engross to 3 modern Es viz. Engineering, Electronics and Energy. They have excelled in these activities. Women entrepreneurs manufacturing solar cookers in Gujarat or owning small foundries in Maharashtra or manufacturing capacitors in Orissa have proved beyond doubt that given the opportunities, they can excel their male counterparts.

In case of Poland, it was found that women entrepreneurs usually begin their businesses to escape unemployment and to gain independence in decision-making. Although male entrepreneurs in Poland face many of the same barriers faced by women entrepreneurs, but the most important barrier to women's participation in Poland's private sector has been the view that women are less pre-destined than men to manage and participate in the country's economic life because of their family obligation.

An investigation of entrepreneurs in the United Kingdom has highlighted that women-owned businesses are proliferating, despite a gap in access to capital. As in other parts of the world, the women in United Kingdom were concerned with getting more education in the areas of business, management and technology issues.

Research among female entrepreneurs in Benin has highlighted the following strong points in their favour: cheap labour, above average technical and intellectual level of women entrepreneurs, investment growth, growing demand for products from Benin, growing awareness of female entrepreneurs for finance and marketing organizations, growing need to form partnerships. However to make dreams come true and to turn visions into reality, certain extra efforts are being explored like monitoring the environment by raising political awareness on this issue, working to make the Benin female economically independent, reassessment of traditional customs and values to sustain the development of women, better credit facilities for women, a better distribution of aid towards female organizations, aid for educating young women, training women entrepreneurs to upgrade marketing and product knowledge, etc.

Bhutan is in the process of transition where more and more women are pursuing higher education and becoming professional/entrepreneurs, but they are still at the nascent stage where exposure to the outside world is limited. Grants received by National Women's Association of Bhutan for the development of women entrepreneurs is utilized to encourage them to plunge into self-employment and for education and training of upcoming women entrepreneurs. The follow-up of this exercise is that the trained entrepreneurs are expected to encourage and train new entrepreneurs.

Conditions necessary for female entrepreneurship are not favorable in Burkina Faso. In order to improve conditions, certain measures have been identified as effective ones: more and better education, training of potential female entrepreneurs in business matters, credit provision without collateral in combination with professional business support, etc.

Although most women-owned businesses are small or medium sized and many operate in the informal sector, they substantially contribute to Costa Rica's economy. However, women's business ventures locally are not regarded as 'business' because they are a necessity for survival. Much of the sprawling informal sector is the direct result of the failure or absence of various public policies ranging from lack of affordable credit to excessive regulatory red tape and corruption. In Costa Rica, many of the challenges that women in business encounter are similar to those which all small businesses face regardless of ownership or gender. These challenges are more complicated for women because of the influences of cultural, ethnic, political and economic biases.

The Philippines experience brings out the following observations: *(a)* In case of highly educated women, the primary motivation for going into business is the professional challenge and/or excitement to prove something to society; *(b)* The higher the education and/or the more experienced the woman becomes, the more she regards the enterprise as an activity that gives social exposure and approval; *(c)* Among poor women who are engaged in entrepreneurial activities as means of survival, they strive to find harmony with their community, which tends to tie them down and make their leap into prosperity a harder option to take. As they are more cautious in individual decision-making, they look to the collective wisdom of their trade group, family or community before taking their businesses one step up in the ladder of growth; *(d)* Women entrepreneurs regard human encounter with market or personal relationships as a major factor in their success. For their size of operation, the more the personal the relationship, the more secure they feel about their business and its potential; *(e)* Women entrepreneurs, who compete for excellence and for a share of market, tend to go into collaborative ventures to address a larger global market. The division of labour is more pronounced, as raw material producers feed into the semi-processed producers, and into the finishers and exporters. The value chain is strengthened for as long as all of them are positioning to the same export market.

Female entrepreneurs in the United States of America enter into business because they want to be in charge of their own destiny or they need more flexibility or are dissatisfied with an unhappy work environment or they have been unchallenged by their present job.

STATUS OF WOMEN ENTREPRENEURS IN INDA

Out of the total 940.48 million people in India, in the 1990's female comprise of 437.10 million representing 46.5 % of the total population. There are 126.48 million women work-force (representing 28.9 per cent of the female population) but as per the1991 census only 185900 women accounting for only 4.5 per cent of total self-employed persons in the country were recorded. Majority of them are engaged in the un-organized sector like agriculture, agro-based industries, handicrafts, handloom and cottage based industries. Participation of women as industrial entrepreneurs however is comparatively a recent phenomenon commencing from 70's era onwards. There were more than 2, 95,680women entrepreneurs claiming 11.2 per cent of total 2.64 million entrepreneurs in India, during 1995-96. This is almost double the percentage of women (5.2%) among the total population of self employed during 1981. On this, a majority was concentrated in low-paid, low-skilled, low-technology and low-productivity jobs in the rural and un-organized sector.

Almost 79.4 million women workers were in the rural areas as against only 10 per cent (86 million) in the urban areas. Only 2.5 million women workers were in the organized sector and a small percentage of 12.4 per cent were total employed. During the 8th, 5 year planning period the number of SSI's expected to rise from 1.7 million to 2.5 million adding 0.8 million in the 5 year period or 1.60 lakh every year. The rough estimate showed that amongst the SSI entrepreneurs' approx. 9 per cent were women entrepreneurs. Their participation however is increasing. Thus considering the trend women participation in another 5 years was more 20 per cent more, raising the number of women entrepreneurs to about 5, 00,000. Therefore one could aim at developing at least 3, 50,000 women entrepreneurs during the 8th, 5 year planning period .through training and other developmental efforts. The present rate of 30 per cent success in EDP training was likely to go up-to 45 per cent with growing experience and improved techniques of training and follow-up. Based on this assumption for getting 3.5 lakh women entrepreneurs it was necessary to train and support about 7.78 lakh entrepreneurs, during the aforesaid period. As per the 2001 census report, there are 22.73 per cent of women workers of the total working population including formal as well as informal sector. In the era of L.P.G (Liberalization, Privatization, Globalization) the Indian women entrepreneurs are very fast entering the non-traditional sectors, which indeed is in response to their greater awareness. Work participation of Indian women is 22 per cent as per 1991 census and triple in rural areas around 27 per cent and in urban areas 9 per cent, thus the role and involvement of women entrepreneurs in rural sector is tremendously enhancing, the literacy levels increased ratio is also a significant factor of this positive trend in the field of entrepreneurship.

PROBLEMS OF WOMEN ENTREPRENEURS IN INDIA

Women in India are faced many problems to get ahead their life in business. A few problems can be detailed as:

1. The greatest deterrent to women entrepreneurs is that they are women. A kind of patriarchal–male dominant social

order is the building block to them in their way towards business success. Male members think it a big risk financing the ventures run by women.

2. The financial institutions are skeptical about the entrepreneurial abilities of women. The bankers consider women loonies as higher risk than men loonies. The bankers put unrealistic and unreasonable securities to get loan to women entrepreneurs. According to a report by the United Nations Industrial Development Organization (UNIDO), "despite evidence that woman's loan repayment rates are higher than men's, women still face more difficulties in obtaining credit," often due to discriminatory attitudes of banks and informal lending groups (UNIDO, 1995b).
3. Entrepreneurs usually require financial assistance of some kind to launch their ventures - be it a formal bank loan or money from a savings account. Women in developing nations have little access to funds, due to the fact that they are concentrated in poor rural communities with few opportunities to borrow money (Starcher, 1996; UNIDO, 1995a). The women entrepreneurs are suffering from inadequate financial resources and working capital. The women entrepreneurs lack access to external funds due to their inability to provide tangible security. Very few women have the tangible property in hand.
4. Women's family obligations also bar them from becoming successful entrepreneurs in both developed and developing nations. "Having primary responsibility for children, home and older dependent family members, few women can devote all their time and energies to their business" (Starcher, 1996) The financial institutions discourage women entrepreneurs on the belief that they can at any time leave their business and become housewives again. The result is that they are forced to rely on their own savings, and loan from relatives and family friends.
5. Indian women give more emphasis to family ties and relationships. Married women have to make a fine balance between business and home. More over the business success

is depends on the support the family members extended to women in the business process and management. The interest of the family members is a determinant factor in the realization of women folk business aspirations.

6. Another argument is that women entrepreneurs have low-level management skills. They have to depend on office staffs and intermediaries, to get things done, especially, the marketing and sales side of business. Here there is more probability for business fallacies like the intermediaries take major part of the surplus or profit. Marketing means mobility and confidence in dealing with the external world, both of which women have been discouraged from developing by social conditioning. Even when they are otherwise in control of an enterprise, they often depend on males of the family in this area.
7. The male:- female competition is another factor, which develop hurdles to women entrepreneurs in the business management process. Despite the fact that women entrepreneurs are good in keeping their service prompt and delivery in time, due to lack of organizational skills compared to male entrepreneurs women have to face constraints from competition. The confidence to travel across day and night and even different regions and states are less found in women compared to male entrepreneurs. This shows the low level freedom of expression and freedom of mobility of the women entrepreneurs.
8. Knowledge of alternative source of raw materials availability and high negotiation skills are the basic requirement to run a business. Getting the raw materials from different souse with discount prices is the factor that determines the profit margin. Lack of knowledge of availability of the raw materials and low-level negotiation and bargaining skills are the factors, which affect women entrepreneur's business adventures.
9. Knowledge of latest technological changes, know how, and education level of the person are significant factor that affect business. The literacy rate of women in India is found

at low level compared to male population. Many women in developing nations lack the education needed to spur successful entrepreneurship. They are ignorant of new technologies or unskilled in their use, and often unable to do research and gain the necessary training (UNIDO, 1995b, p.1). Although great advances are being made in technology, many women's illiteracy, structural difficulties, and lack of access to technical training prevent the technology from being beneficial or even available to females ("Women Entrepreneurs in Poorest Countries," 2001). According to The Economist, this lack of knowledge and the continuing treatment of women as second-class citizens keep them in a pervasive cycle of poverty ("The Female Poverty Trap," 2001). The studies indicate that uneducated women don't have the knowledge of measurement and basic accounting.

10. Low-level risk taking attitude is another factor affecting women folk decision to get into business. Low-level education provides low-level self-confidence and self-reliance to the women folk to engage in business, which is continuous risk taking and strategic cession making profession. Investing money, maintaining the operations and ploughing back money for surplus generation requires high risk taking attitude, courage and confidence. Though the risk tolerance ability of the women folk in day-to-day life is high compared to male members, while in business it is found opposite to that.

11. Achievement motivation of the women folk found less compared to male members. The low level of education and confidence leads to low level achievement and advancement motivation among women folk to engage in business operations and running a business concern.

12. Finally high production cost of some business operations adversely affects the development of women entrepreneurs. The installation of new machineries during expansion of the productive capacity and like similar factors dissuades the women entrepreneurs from venturing into new areas.

HOW TO DEVELOP WOMEN ENTREPRENEURSs?

Right efforts on from all areas are required in the development of women entrepreneurs and their greater participation in the entrepreneurial activities. Following efforts can be taken into account for effective development of women entrepreneurs:

1. Consider women as specific target group for all developmental programmes.
2. Better educational facilities and schemes should be extended to women folk from government part.
3. Adequate training programme on management skills to be provided to women community.
4. Encourage women's participation in decision-making.
5. Vocational training to be extended to women community that enables them to understand the production process and production management.
6. Skill development to be done in women's polytechnics and industrial training institutes. Skills are put to work in training-cum-production workshops.
7. Training on professional competence and leadership skill to be extended to women entrepreneurs.
8. Training and counseling on a large scale of existing women entrepreneurs to remove psychological causes like lack of self-confidence and fear of success.
9. Counseling through the aid of committed NGOs, psychologists, managerial experts and technical personnel should be provided to existing and emerging women entrepreneurs.
10. Continuous monitoring and improvement of training programmes.
11. Activities in which women are trained should focus on their marketability and profitability.
12. Making provision of marketing and sales assistance from government part.

13. To encourage more passive women entrepreneurs the Women training programme should be organized that taught to recognize her own psychological needs and express them.
14. State finance corporations and financing institutions should permit by statute to extend purely trade related finance to women entrepreneurs.
15. Women's development corporations have to gain access to open-ended financing.
16. The financial institutions should provide more working capital assistance both for small scale venture and large scale ventures.
17. Making provision of micro credit system and enterprise credit system to the women entrepreneurs at local level.
18. Repeated gender sensitization programs should be held to train financiers to treat women with dignity and respect as persons in their own right.
19. Infrastructure, in the form of industrial plots and sheds, to set up industries is to be provided by state run agencies.
20. Industrial estates could also provide marketing outlets for the display and sale of products made by women.
21. A Women Entrepreneur's Guidance Cell set up to handle the various problems of women entrepreneurs all over the state.
22. District Industries Centers and Single Window Agencies should make use of assisting women in their trade and business guidance.
23. Programs for encouraging entrepreneurship among women are to be extended at local level.
24. Training in entrepreneurial attitudes should start at the high school level through well-designed courses, which build confidence through behavioral games.
25. More governmental schemes to motivate women entrepreneurs to engage in small scale and large-scale business ventures.

26. Involvement of Non Governmental Organizations in women entrepreneurial training programs and counseling.

CONCLUSION

Independence brought promise of equality of opportunity in all sphere to the Indian women and laws guaranteeing for their equal rights of participation in political process and equal opportunities and rights in education and employment were enacted. But unfortunately, the government sponsored development activities have benefited only a small section of women. The large majority of them are still unaffected by change and development activities have benefited only a small section of women i.e. the urban middle class women. The large majority of them are still unaffected by change and development. The reasons are well sighted in the discussion part of this article. It is hoped that the suggestions forwarded in the article will help the entrepreneurs in particular and policy-planners in general to look into this problem and develop better schemes, developmental programmes and opportunities to the women folk to enter into more entrepreneurial ventures. This article here tries to recollect some of the successful women entrepreneurs like EktaKapoor, Creative Director, Balaji Telefilms, KiranMazumdar Shaw, CEO, Biocon, Shahnaz Husain and Vimalben M Pawale, Ex President, Sri MahilaGrihaUdyogLijjatPapad (SMGULP).

REFERENCES

1. Women Entrepreneurship and Economic Development—By Sanjay Tiwari, AnshujaTiwari. Publisher : SarupandSons
2. Entrepreneurship Development—By S.S Khanka. S. Chand & Company Limited. (Ram Nagar, New Delhi-110055).
3. Dynamics of Entrepreneurial Development and Management—By Vasant Desai. Himalaya Publishing House.
4. Indian Entrepreneurship (Theory and Practice)- By Dr. D.D. Sharma & Dr. S.K. Dhameja Abhishek Publications Chandigarh-17 (India)
5. Internet Related Search Topics—Danish Agency for Trade and Industry October 2000, Electronic Edition by Schultz Grafisk A/S.

6. Alvarez, S.A., and Meyer, G.D. (1998). Why Do Women Become Entrepreneurs? *Frontiers of Entrepreneurship Research*, Wellesley, MA: Babson College.

7. Anna, A.L., Chandler, G. N., Jansen, E., and Mero, N. P. (2000). Women Business Owners in Traditional and Non-Traditional Industries," *Journal of Business Venturing.*

8. Ben-Yoseph, M., Gundry, L.K., and Maslyk-Musial, E. (1994). Women Entrepreneurs in the United States and Poland, *Kobieta I Biznes.*

9. Ben-Yoseph, M., and Gundry, L.K. (1997). Teaching About Women Managers and Women Entrepreneurs Across Cultures, *Journal of Developmental Entrepreneurship.*

10. Birley, Sue (1989). Female entrepreneurs; Are They Really Different? *Journal of Small Business Management*, Summer.

11. Brush, C. (1992). Research on Women Business Owners: Past Trends, A New Perspective and Future Directions, *Entrepreneurship: Theory and Practice.*

12. Brush, C. (1997). Women-owned Businesses: Obstacles and Opportunities, *Journal of* Developmental Entrepreneurship.*

13. Brush, C., and Hisrich, R. (1988). Women Entrepreneurs: Strategic Origins Impact on Growth. *Frontiers of Entrepreneurship Research.* Wellesley, MA: Babson College.

14. Clark, T., and James, F. (1992). Women-owned Businesses: Dimensions and Policy Issues. *Economic Development Quarterly.*

15. Gundry, L.K., and Welsch, H.P. (1994). Differences in Familial Influence Among Women-Owned Businesses. Family Business Review.

16. Hisrich, R., Brush, C., Good, D., and DeSouza, G. (1997). Performance in Entrepreneurial Ventures. Does Gender Matter? Frontiers of Entrepreneurship Research. Wellesley, MA: Babson College.

2

Entrepreneurs Attitude Towards Investment Decision

Dr. Aravind.S
Dr. Santosh Singh Bais

ABSTRACT

Entrepreneurship is a complex and multifaceted phenomenon and it is gaining importance in many countries around the world. The changing nature of the business and the world in which it operates make entrepreneurial behaviour influential. Change is pertinent in today's world and change creates opportunities for the entrepreneurial class. The exploding industry sector has opened up exciting opportunities. The increased prevalence of outsourcing by many business operations is creating new opportunities for entrepreneurs. The blurring of national borders, the encouragement to world trade and the increasing availability of information has opened up international opportunities to entrepreneurs. Present day entrepreneurs face new and different challenges like increasing concern for social good, information technology, ever changing internal and external environment, development of communication technology, and increasing competition.

Key words Entrepreneurship, Attitudes, Investment Decisions etc.,

INTRODUCTION

Entrepreneurship is a complex and multifaceted phenomenon and it is gaining importance in many countries around the world. The changing nature of the business and the world in which it operates make entrepreneurial behaviour influential. Change is pertinent in today's world and change creates opportunities for the entrepreneurial class. The exploding industry sector has opened up exciting opportunities. The increased prevalence of outsourcing by many business operations is creating new opportunities for entrepreneurs. The blurring of national borders, the encouragement to world trade and the increasing availability of information has opened up international opportunities to entrepreneurs. Present day entrepreneurs face new and different challenges like increasing concern for social good, information technology, ever changing internal and external environment, development of communication technology, and increasing competition.

Becoming an entrepreneur is a challenging task and it needs qualities like knowledge, attitude, skills, initiative, drive and perception. Attitude plays a vital role among the qualities, which include openness, risk assumption, effective task execution and so on. Attitude is a word used commonly and loosely. It differs among individuals because each entrepreneur is unique. For instance, the attitude for investing money in business differs from one to another, which is an important human behaviour. Attitudes are formed or acquired with various objects, people and environment. In other words, Attitude is the detailed direction of human behaviour, state of sensitiveness and prone to act.

In this rapidly changing world, entrepreneur should be able to change his attitude and his approaches depending on the prevailing environment. Changing attitude is tough as there can be innumerable hurdles to acquire the change. Attitude towards things, change under various circumstances. Bringing a change in attitude is favourable if the end result is good. They should carefully pla`X`n and develop a futuristic frame of reference from which to identify potential opportunities and threats, and take action to exploit the opportunities as well as defend against threats. The quality of decisions depends on individual's attitude towards particular actions/decisions.

Good decision making ability is the key to business success. It is an intellectual activity involving careful study and critical evaluation of various options and finally selecting the most appropriate one using sound judgement. Of all the decisions, the investment decision occupies a pre-dominant role in financial management. Today's environment is complex, dynamic and challenging. At this juncture, the entrepreneur should have ability to manage its investment that requires knowledge of investment, markets and instruments as well as an understanding of the various factors that affect the investment performance and how they all interact. This study takes into cognition all the above mentioned, in particular the attitude of an individual in taking the investment decisions.

STATEMENT OF THE PROBLEM

Investment plays a vital role in the overall and continuous process of economic development. In fact, the quantum of investment decides the process and direction of growth of any institution/organisation with business motives.

Taking the investment decision is among the business' most difficult decisions any entrepreneur encounters. It requires special attention because it has a long-range impact on the business performance and they are critical to the business success or failure. The fundamental objectives of any investment decision are survival and growth, though there could be other social objectives too such as social status or social responsibility, employment for self and or others and so on. These objectives depend on one's potential and his state of mind at that time.

OBJECTIVES OF THE STUDY

The Present study has following objectives

1. To identify the entrepreneurs profile to match the mind set

2. To examine the attitudes influencing investment decisions
3. To find out the risk tolerance of the entrepreneurs
4. To identify the entrepreneurs profile to match the mind set
5. To examine the attitudes influencing investment decisions
6 To find out the risk tolerance of the entrepreneurs

The researcher relied heavily on primary data. The required data was collected from the entrepreneurs doing business in the Raichur city. The study was conducted in the month of August and September 2010 through self-administered questionnaire. The sample size covered 56 entrepreneurs who were spread through different locations in the above area, which was chosen for researcher convenience. The collected data has been analysed through the application of statistical tools such as rank correlation, Standard deviation, correlation, and simple percentage analysis.

Small scale industrial enterprises form the backbone of an economy. They offer good employment opportunities, nurture the locally available entrepreneurial skills, help in balance growth, and improve the overall economic conditions.

SCOPE OF THE STUDY

This study is confined to entrepreneurs doing business in Raichur city. Since the objective of this study is to find out the influence of attitudes in the minds of entrepreneurs who take investment decisions, the other factors which influence investment decisions is not taken into account. Depending on need, the finding of this study can be used by industrial houses, academicians and incompetent decision-makers. The findings may also be beneficial for general public and future prospective entrepreneurs.

RESEARCH METHODOLOGY

The researcher relied heavily on primary data. The required data was collected from the entrepreneurs doing business in the Raichur city. The study was conducted in the month of August and September 2010 through self-administered questionnaire.

The sample size covered 56 entrepreneurs who were spread through different locations in the above area, which was chosen for researcher convenience. The collected data has been analysed through the application of statistical tools such as rank correlation, standard deviation, correlation, and simple percentage analysis.

REVIEW OF LITERATURE

There are several examples of engineers' technocrats and other professionals who have pioneered new ventures and proved to be an outstanding success as entrepreneurs. Udai Pareek (1983) discuss that based on interviews of selected chief—executives—all of whom except one having professional background- probes into the life styles, social values and other characteristics of these professionals — turned-industrialists. Howard E Van Auken and Lynn Neeley (1998) examine the relationship between pre-launch planning and the acquisition of start-up for a sample of 78 small firms. Specifically, the study investigates the relationship between planning and *(a)* the size of initial capitalisation; *(b)* percentage of start up equity in initial capital structure; (c) use of bootstrap financing; and *(d)* difficulty of raising start-up capital.

Maryann P Feldman and Johanna Francis (2000) outlines the development of a high-tech industrial cluster through the efforts of entrepreneurs who adapted to both constructive crises and new opportunities, creating the factors and conditions that facilitated their business interests. They examine the initial factors influencing individual decisions to become entrepreneurs and how external factors influence the formation and location of high technology clusters. The perspective taken is that entrepreneurs are a critical element in the formation of clusters and their actions are important in the analysis of clusters as complex adaptive systems.

Saras D Saravathy (2001) attempts to see if there are some common elements that different entrepreneurs share and if there is a unique way the entrepreneurs think. It highlights the differences between 'effectual' reasoning which is mostly used by the entrepreneurs, and 'causal' reasoning which is more often used in business by professional managers. Garry Knight (2000) investigates the impact of entrepreneurial orientation on the performance of small and medium sized firms in the globalised context while competing with the multinational companies. The author constructs a hypothetical model and tests the hypotheses with a market survey of small and medium firms from industries such as electronics and electrical equipments, textiles and apparel related products, which have been affected more by the forces of globalisation than some other industries. David Hillson and Ruth Murray-Webster (2004) states that the inability og usual risk management practices to avoid project failures demands structured and matured processes to counter projects risks. It is the attitude of the members and organisation which has a significant impact on the delivery of effective risk management practices and it is emotional intelligence that emphasises importance of the human element and focuses on developing risk attitudes that ensure project success.

FEATURES OF THE SAMPLE POPULATION

The researcher has collected opinion from 53 male and 3 female respondents. All are married. As regards the educational levèl of respondents, it has been classified into four categories viz. School level, Under Graduate, Post Graduate and Professionals. There are 14 professionals, 14 under graduates, 22 school level and the rest post graduates.

In the age group concern, of the 56 respondents, 23 fall under 'between 31-40' , 16 respondents fall under 'between 41-50', 11 respondents fall under 'between below 30', and the rest fall under 'between 51 and above'. This has been presented in Table 2.1 and Graph 2.1.

Table 2.1: Distribution of Respondents—Age and Sex Wise

Sex/Age	Below 30	31-40	41-50	51 & above
Male	09	21	16	06
Female	02	02	–	–
Total	**11**	**23**	**16**	**06**

Graph 2.1 Distribution of The Respondents Education Level

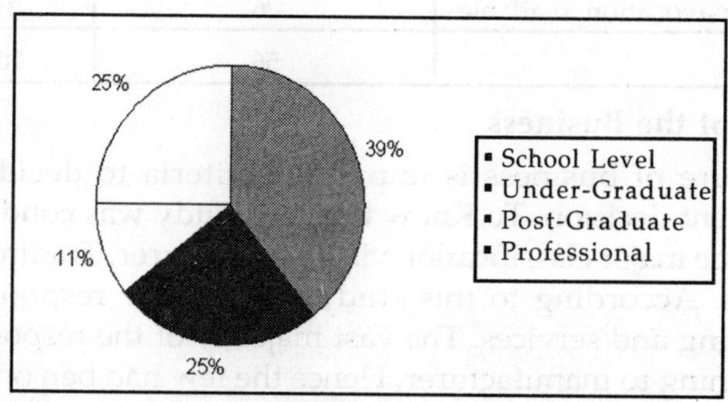

RESULTS

The purpose of this chapter is to examine the attitudes influencing investment decisions. Keeping the above as a primary objective, the questionnaire was designed and the collected data were analysed as under:

INSTITUTION OWNED BY

To examine the attitude of entrepreneurs, the first step is to know the institution belongs to first generation or hereditary. According to this study, 82 per cent of the respondents are belonging to first generation and the rest belongs to hereditary. The questions were asked to first generation entrepreneurs, the reasons for becoming entrepreneurs. This result has been discussed as under.

REASONS FOR BECOMING ENTREPRENEURS

In this study was conducted to know the reasons for becoming entrepreneurs. According to this study, 78.56 per cent of the respondents reveal that the self confidence is the primary factor for becoming entrepreneur, and the rest equally divided into family coercion and no other avocation available. The data has been furnished in the Table 2.2

Table 2.2: Reasons for Becoming Entrepreneur

Reasons	No. of Respondent	Percent
Self-confidence	44	78.56
Family coercion	06	10.72
No other avocation available	06	10.72
Total	**56**	**100.00**

Nature of the Business

Nature of business is important criteria to decide the investment decision. To Know this, the study was conducted with three major classification viz. Manufacturer, Trading and Services. According to this study, a very few respondents are trading and services. The vast majority of the respondent are beloning to manufacturer. Hence the few had ben omitted the mojoirty has taken into account.

Initial Investment

This is one of the more important and diffcult issues facing entrepreneures. According to this study. the average initial investment of the repondents is 5.75 lakh and the deviation is 10.07.

Mode of Financing

One of the major issues faced by the enterpreneneur is that of mobilising funds. According to this research study, 32 per cent of the respondents started business from their own sources, 25 per cent of the respondents from own plus bank assistant, 21 per cent of the respondents from bank assistance and the rest from own plus friends and relatives. The data has been indicated in table 2.3

Tenure of the Investment Decision

Tenure of the investment decisions depend on the objectives of the entrepreneurs. It differs with one another and time horizon. The research study shows that 43 per cent

Table 2.3: Mode of Funding for Initial Investment

Mode	No. of Respondent	Percent
Own Sources	18	32.14
Bank Assistance	12	21.43
Own+Bank Assistance	14	25.00
Own plus Friends & Relatives	10	17.86
Venture Capital	02	03.57
Total	**56**	**100.00**

Field Survey

of the respondents are taking medium term investment decisions, 32 per cent of the respondents are taking long term and the rest in short term. The data has been furnished in table 2.4.

Table 2.4: Tenure of Investment Decision

Period	No. of Respondents	Percent
Short-term	14	25.00
Medium-term	24	42.86
Long-term	18	32.14
Total	**56**	**100.00**

Field Survey

Mode of Working Capital

Working capital is the life blood of every business especially in manufacturing sector. The firm should maintain a sound working capital position. It should have adequate working capital to run the business operations. Both excessive as well as inadequate working capital positions re dangerous from the firm's point of view. Maintaining the optimum level is challenging task and it depends on the sources. To know the mode of working capital, the questions were asked to the respondents, the responses as follows. Of the 56 respondents, 34 are using the own sources for working capital and 16 respondents from banks and the rest in sundry creditors. The data has been depicted in the Graph 2.2.

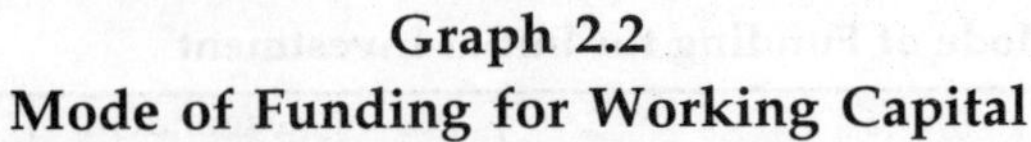

Graph 2.2
Mode of Funding for Working Capital

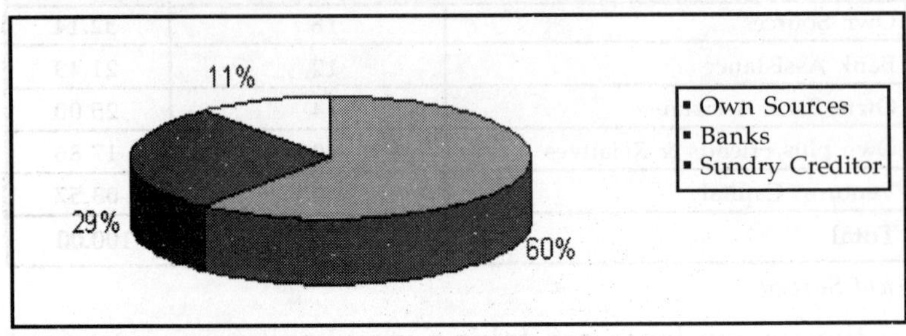

Awareness about Factoring Services

Credit management is a specialised activity, and involves a lot of time and effort of a company. Collection of receivables poses a problem, particularly for small scale enterprises. Factoring is a unique financial innovation. It is both a financial as well as a management support to a client. It is a popular mechanism of managing, financing and collection receivables in developed countries like USA and UK, and have extended to a number other countries in the recent past, including India. A company can assign its credit management and collection to specialist organisation called factoring organisations. Keeping the above as objective, the questions were asked to the respondents, 71 per cent of the respondents reveal that they do not have the awareness about the factoring service and the rest know and using factoring services namely Canbank and Sundaram factoring services. The data has been stated in graph 2.3.

No. of Years in Business and Nature of the Investment Decisions

Small firm investment decisions is strongly influenced, and to large extent characterised, by the inherent competencies of the entrepreneur. 54 per cent of the respondents' investment decision were expansion of their business and 29 per cent of the respondents' investment decisions were modernisation of the business. This is because of majority of the respondents were doing business less than 10 years. The data has been depicted in table 2.5.

Graph 2.3
Awareness About Factoring

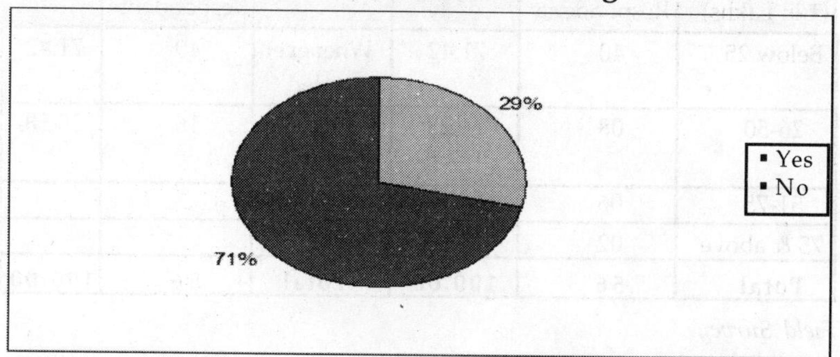

Table 2.5: No. of Year in Current Business and Nature of Investment

In Year	No. of Respondents	Per Cent	Nature of Decisions	No. of Respondents	Per Cent
Below 5	24	42.86	Expansion	30	53.57
6-10	20	35.71	Modernisation	16	28.57
11-15	04	07.14	Replacement	06	10.71
16 & above	08	14.29	Diversification	04	07.15
Total	**56**	**100.00**	**Total**	**56**	**100.00**

Field Survey

Turnover and Frequency of Investment Decisions

Investment decisions depend on the firms' financial positions and it decides the frequency of investment decisions. According to this study, 71 per cent of the respondents fall under 'below 25', 15 per cent of the respondents fall under 'between 26-50', 11 per cent of the respondents fall under ' 51-75', and the rest fall under '75 and above'. The frequency of the investment decisions regards, 71 per cent of the respondent reveals that they took whenever the situation warrants and the rest took as regular budgeted.

Influencing Factors of the Investment Decisions

Before taking the investment decisions, the entrepreneurs should consider the various factors like price of raw material, price of product, Product demand, government policies,

Table 2.6: Turnover and Frequency of Investment Decision

Turnover (₹ in Lakhs)	No. of Respondents	Per cent	Frequency	No. of Respondents	Per cent
Below 25	40	71.42	Whenever needed	40	71.42
26-50	08	14.28	As regular Budgeted	16	28.58
51-75	06	10.72			
75 & above	02	03.58			
Total	**56**	**100.00**	**Total**	**56**	**100.00**

Field Survey

technological changes, product life and entry of competitors. To know which factors influencing more in investment decisions, the questions were asked to the respondents to rank the influencing factor according to them. According to this study, Technological changes and entry new competitors were ranked highest by the respondents.

DISCUSSIONS

The majority of the Entrepreneurs start their companies after acquiring the same industry experience. The reason behind that they did not get proper recognition, rewards, and so on. These factors boosted their confidence level and they started the business. The most of the investment decisions are expansion and modernisation. It is because of no. of years in the current business and their turnover of the business. It is evidence by those whose initial capital is more as well as 15 years of experience of the business. Though the bank and creditors mode are utilised for working capital, that has to be improved further and try to utilise the factoring services. Those who are having turnover less than 25 lakhs, their investment decisions were made the situation warrants not in a regular basis. This shows that the entrepreneurs do not have risk taking attitude towards investment decisions on regular budgeted basis and also turnover and entry competitors.

FINDINGS

From the above results and discussions, the researcher identified the followings:

1. Institutions owned by the first generation entrepreneurs are having prior experience on the same area.
2. Majority of the investment decisions are medium term.
3. Most of the investment decisions are expansion and modernisation.
4. Few of them are having habits to take investment decisions are regular budgeted manner.
5. 60 per cent of the respondents mode of working capital is own sources.
6. Technological changes and entry competitors influences their investment decisions.

CONCLUSION

Small scale industrial enterprises form the backbone of an economy. They offer good employment opportunities, nurture the locally available entrepreneurial skills, help in balance growth, and improve the overall economic conditions. However it is widely accepted that investment decisions influenced their success or failure of the business due to various factors. This chapter examines about the attitudes towards investment decisions. The results evidence on the relationship between the attitude and investment decisions. Though they have confidence on their decisions, many of them were hesitating to provide regular budget for investment decisions due to various reasons.

REFERENCES

1. Ahuja. K.K, (1991), "Industrial Psychology and Organisational Behaviour" First Edition, Chapter 11, pp 86-100.
2. David Hillson and Ruth Murrary-Webster, (2004) "Understanding and Managing Risk Attitude", www.risk-doctor.com.
3. Garry Kinght (2000), "Entrepreneurship and Marketing Stratergy: The SME Under Globalisation", Journal of International Marketing, Vol.8, No.2, pp 12-32.

4. Howard E Van Auken and Lynn Neeley (2004)," The Impact of Planning on the Acquisition of Start-up", ICFAI Journal of Entrepreneurship Development, Vol.1 No.3, pp 57-65.

5. Maryaan P Feldman and Johanna Francis (2004)," Entrepreneurs and the Formation of Industrial Clusters" ICFAI Journal of Entrepreneurship Development, Vol.1 No.2, pp 39-56.

6. Panday I.M (2009), "Financial Management', 9th Edition, Vikas Publications Limited, Chapter 8, pp 141-158.

7. Saras D Sarasvathy (2004)," Entrepreneurs and the Formation of Industrial Clusters" ICFAI Journal of Entrepreneurship Development, Vol.1 No.2, pp 57-65.

8. Udai Pareek (1983), "A Profile of Organisational Entrepreneurs", Indian Management, Vol. 22 No.10, pp 7-9.

3

Women Entrepreneurship
Challenges and Opportunities

Dr. Jiwan Jhunjhunwale

ABSTRACT

Entrepreneurship refers to the dynamic process of organizing, managing and assuming the risk of a business. It refers to the activity of searching for change, responding to it and exploiting it as an opportunity. Entrepreneurship is undertaken to initiate, maintain or organize a profit oriented business unit for the production and distribution of economic goods and services. Entrepreneurial growth in India is as old as Rig-veda but there was no manufacturing as such before 1850. This manufacturing entrepreneurship was too confined to cottage and small scale industry. The true industrial development took place after independence since indigenous entrepreneurship was no longer requiring functioning as the camp followers of foreign interests.

Women entrepreneurs are key players in any developing country particularly in terms of their contribution to economic development. In recent years, even among the developed countries like USA and Canada, Women's role in terms of their share in small business has been increasing. Indian women have increasing opportunities like, higher levels of education, economic compulsions, constitutional right to guarantee them equal opportunities, gender equality through empowerment of women, economic empowerment etc. There are umpteen problems faced by women at various stages beginning from their initial commencement of the enterprise, in running their enterprise. Sustainable growth and development in entrepreneurship can be achieved if resources (human or non–human) are fully exploited.

A number of plans, policies and programmes have been drawn up by the government to ensure greater opportunities to women entrepreneurs. Women are willing to take up business ad contribute to the nation's growth. Their role is also being recognized and steps are being taken to promote women entrepreneurship. Resurgence of entrepreneurship is the need of hour. Women entrepreneurs must be molded properly with entrepreneurial traits and skills to meet changing trends and challenging global markets, and also be competent enough to sustain and strive in the local economic arena. Increase in women entrepreneurship activities will logically led to generation of more income, reduction in unemployment, minimization of poverty, reduction regional imbalances, increase in export trade and reduction of balance of payment to a certain extent.

INTRODUCTION

Entrepreneurship refers to the dynamic process of organizing, managing and assuming the risk of a business. It refers to the activity of searching for change, responding to it and exploiting it as an opportunity. Entrepreneurship is undertaken to initiate, maintain or organize a profit oriented business unit for the production and distribution of economic goods and services.

Entrepreneurial growth in India is as old as Rig-veda but there was no manufacturing as such before 1850. This manufacturing entrepreneurship was too confined to cottage and small scale industry. But it could not grow further due to various reasons like political ununity, lack of capital, network of custom barriers, existence of multiple systems of currency. Swadeshi movement in 1905 attempt to revive indigenous goods and this attempt gave a boost to Indian entrepreneurship. J.R.D Tata established its steel unit in Jamshedpur in 1911. After First World War, Indian and British enterprisers came to interpenetrate in many common fields and industries. The managing agency system came into existence. The true industrial development took place after independence since indigenous entrepreneurship was no longer requiring functioning as the camp followers of foreign interests. To overcome inflation, to attain economic security and to produce a stimulating climate for industry, the government of India announced Industrial Policy in 1948 followed by five year plans with many changes which were introduced from time to time.

As put by Sakuntala Narasimhan, a Journalist, "It is awareness, rather than conventional schooling or education in terms of degree of classrooms that makes a vital difference." Empowerment, in real sense, does not necessarily mean living in midst of material comforts in luxurious palace. Women powerless in self–assertion or autonomy over her own life is powerless as a slave. Increase in autonomy, right of decision making and entitlements in terms of dignity etc. may be taken as yardsticks of progresses and 'development 'of women. The overall picture is to use a smile, like a half- filled glass—one can either look at the half that is full, and take the pleasure in the fact that it is filled, or look at the half that is empty and spotlight bravely what remains to be done. In such a scenario, both the assessments are true. Fortunately, Indian women, their progress, aspirations, foresightedness, goals etc. belongs to the former part of the picture. Indian women are today better off economically, socially, politically, psychologically than they were at the time of independence.

Women Entrepreneurs

Women entrepreneurs are key players in any developing country particularly in terms of their contribution to economic development. In recent years, even among the developed countries like USA and Canada, Women's role in terms of their share in small business has been increasing. The facts of a study conducted by IIT, Delhi is:

(i) Women own one – third of small business in USA and Canada.

(ii) Britain has seen an increase of over three times of women in work force than that of men even since 1980s.

(iii) Women make for 40% of total work force in Asian Countries.

(iv) In China women outnumber men by at least two times when it comes to starting business there.

(v) In Japan, the percentage of women entrepreneurs increased from 2.4 Per cent in 1980 to 5.2 Per cent in 1995.

We may think that Indian women cannot be good entrepreneur but the myth that Indian women cannot go beyond home has been convincingly demolished by modern age. As women are migrating to towns and cities, there is education and economic Independence. Doors are opening giving her access to areas where she can growth and blossom as a person in her own right. Indian women have boldly invaded the wither to forbidden land of entrepreneurship taken to risk, faced the challenges and proved to world that socially, politically, psychologically, they are not more merely at the receiving end. A section of urban women emerged as potential entrepreneurs. Women do have vast entrepreneurial talent which can be harnessed to convert them from the position of job seeker to job givers. Entrepreneurship itself has been recognized as a fully fledged profession and women entrepreneurship is an even newer phenomenon in India.

Indian women have increasing opportunities like, higher levels of education, economic compulsions, constitutional right to guarantee them equal opportunities, gender equality through empowerment of women, economic empowerment etc. Women also have desires and also aspire to enter and succeed in all fields at par with men. The above said argument is confirmed by the facts that the number of women is technical, professional, engineering streams has been increasing. For instance, potential women entrepreneurs have increased from 6000 in 1950 -51 to 3, 28,000 in 1996-97. But in spite of their aspirations, Indian women are far behind than women entrepreneurs of other countries like Japan and China. Indian women entrepreneurs started their entrepreneurial work in 1970s but are still not at par with women entrepreneurs of China and Japan where the entrepreneurial work started mainly in 1980s. Polytechnics and ITI's have only 15 per cent girls out of total enrolled students. And those who join or set their own enterprisers is still less in number. The reason is not one but many.

PROBLEMS OF WOMEN ENTREPRENEURS

There are umpteen problems faced by women at various stages beginning from their initial commencement of the enterprise, in running their enterprise. Their various problems are as follows:

Patriarchal Society: Entrepreneurship has been traditionally seen as a male preserve and idea of women taking up entrepreneurial activities is considered as a distant dream. Any deviation from the norm is frowned up and if possible, immediately curbed. Women also have to face role conflict as soon as they initiate any entrepreneurial activity. It is an uphill task for women to face such conflicts and cope with the twin role.

Absence of Entrepreneurial Aptitude: Many women take the training by attending the Entrepreneurship Development Programme's without an entrepreneurial bent of mind. As per a study, involvement of women in the small scale sector as owners stands at mere 7 %. Women who are imparted training by various institutes must be verified on account of aptitude through the tests, interviews etc.

Quality of EDPs: All women entrepreneurs are given the same training through EDPs. Second-generation women entrepreneurs don't such training as they already have the previous exposure to business.

Marketing Problems: Women entrepreneurs continuously face the problems in marketing their products. It is one of the core problems as this area is mainly dominated by males and even women with adequate experience fail to make a dent.

For marketing the products women entrepreneurs have to be at the mercy of middlemen who pocket the chunk of profit. Although the middlemen exploit the women entrepreneurs, the elimination of middlemen is difficult, because it involves a lot of running about. Women entrepreneurs also find it difficult to capture the market and make their products popular.

Financial Problems: Obtaining the support of bankers, managing the working capital, lack of credit resources are the problems which still remain in the male domain. Women are yet to make significant mark in quantitative terms. Marketing and financial problems are such obstacles where even training doesn't significantly help the women. Some problems are structural in nature and beyond the control of entrepreneurs.

Family Conflicts: Women also face the conflict of performing of home role as they are not available to spend enough time with their families. They spend long hours in business and as a result, they find it difficult to meet the demands of their family members and society as well. Their inability to attend to domestic work, time for education of children, personal hobbies, and entertainment adds to their conflicts.

Credit Facilities: Though women constitute about 50 % of population, the percentage of small scale enterprise where women own 51 % of share capital is less than 5 %. Women are often denied credit by bankers on the ground of lack of collateral security. Therefore, women's access to risk capital is limited.

The complicated procedure of bank loans, the inordinate delay in obtaining the loans and running about involved do deter many women from venturing out. At the same time, a good deal of self- employment programme has been promoted by the govt and commercial banks.

Shortage of raw–materials: Women entrepreneurs encounter the problems of shortage of raw materials. The failure of many women co-operations in 1971 such as these engaged in basket making were mainly because of the inadequate availability of forest based raw materials.

Heavy C competition: Many of the women enterprisers have imperfect organizational set up. But they have to face severe competition from organized industries.

High Cost of production: High cost of production undermines the efficiency and stands in the way of development and expansion of women's enterprises. Government assistance in the form of grant and subsidies to some extent enables them to tide over the difficult situations. However, in the long run, it would be necessary to increase efficiency and expand productive capacity and thereby reduce cost to make their ultimate survival possible. Other than these, women entrepreneurs also face the problems of labor, human resources, infrastructure, legal formalities, overload of work, lack of family support, mistrust etc.

"When woman moves forward, the family moves, the village moves and the nation moves" this is rightly said by Pandit Jawahar Neheru. Employment gives status and economic independence to women leading to an empowered woman.

Women set up an enterprise due to economic and non — economic reasons as well. Various reasons can be due to *(i)* Motivational factors; *(ii)* Facilitating factors.

MOTIVATIONAL FACTORS

- Economic Necessity
- Self – actualization
- Independence
- Govt. Policies & Programmes
- Education & Qualification
- Role model to others
- Employment Generation
- Self identity & Social Status
- Success stories of friends & relatives
- Family Occupation

FACILITATING FACTORS

- Adequate Financial Facilities
- Self – Satisfaction
- Innovative Thinking
- Network of contacts
- Co-operation of family
- Experienced and skilled people at work
- Support of family members.

STEPS TAKEN BY THE GOVERNMENT

Sustainable growth and development in entrepreneurship can be achieved if resources (human or non–human) are fully exploited. A number of plans, policies and programmes have been drawn up by the govt. to ensure greater opportunities to women entrepreneurs. Some of the activities/policies of government are:

- The Department of women and child Development, Ministry of Human Resource Development had launched a special campaign for capturing women's work in 1991 census.

- Under the scheme of Prime Minister's Rozar Yojana, women oriented schemes of SFCs, IDBI, KVIC, etc, women beneficiaries are granted loans. KVIC has been stretched its wings to a group of women in the sunder bans region of West Bengal. KVIC is providing interest–free loans for Muslim spinning to these handfuls of women who set up a society in 1981 under the direct list of KVIC.

- The Rashtriya Mahila Kosh was set up in 1983 to provide micro-credit to poor women who had no access to financial institutions at reasonable rates of interest, with very low transaction costs and simple procedures.

- The Government has started Training Programmes exclusively for self-employment of women through various schemes such as Support for Training and Employment Programme of women (STEP), setting up training cum employment cum-production units (NORAD), Development of women and children in rural areas (DWCRA).

- A Number of agencies like National Institute of small Industry extension Training, (NISIET), Small Industry service Institutes (SISI), State Financial Corporation's (SFCs), National Small Industries Corporations (NSICs), NABARD etc. Conduct EDPs to train women entrepreneurs and their follow-up.
- Separate Cells in these agencies are set up women who provide counseling and follow up services to women entrepreneurs. They also assist women entrepreneurs in their project selection, project preparation, escort services to ensure its sanction and launch.
- District Industries Centers (DICs) have been asked by Haryana govt. to organize lectures, seminars in girls colleges, technical institutes to encourage them set up enterprises.
- University Grants Commission (UGC) has made the subject of entrepreneurship as a mandatory part of curriculum in the educational institutions.
- Women's Development Corporations have been set up by many states to evolve strategies for women's development.
- SIDBI is running the Mahila Udyog Nidhi and Mahila Vikas Yojana for offering development assistance.

Women are willing to take up business ad contribute to the nation's growth. Their role is also being recognized and steps are being taken to promote women entrepreneurship. Resurgence of entrepreneurship is the need of hour. Women entrepreneurs must be moulded properly with entrepreneurial traits and skills to meet changing trends and challenging global markets, and also be competent enough to sustain and strive in the local economic arena.

CONCLUSION

Women constitute 50 per cent of the total population. This unutilized active population can be converted into effective entrepreneurs. No doubt they face large number of problems and challenges in the due course of management of their enterprises. Due to globalization and liberalization new opportunities will certainly come on their way and those who will grab those opportunities they will certainly carve a place for themselves in this professionally driven entrepreneurship world. Increase in women entrepreneurship activities will logically led to generation of more income, reduction in unemployment, minimization of poverty, reduction regional imbalances, increase in export trade and reduction of balance of payment to a certain extent.

SHAHNAZ HUSAIN—A SUCCESSFUL WOMEN ENTREPRENEUR:

Shahnaz Husain a well known name in herbal cosmetics hails from a conservative Muslim family. She is pioneer in herbal cosmetics not only in India but the world over. She has been acclaimed to be the "World's Greatest Women Entrepreneur" due to her extraordinary contribution in herbal market. She has already grabbed 80 per cent of domestic herbal market and owns multiple chain stores in developed countries like Japan, US, England and as so on. Married at a very young age of 15 years Shahnaz Husain had an urge to becomes something more than a mere housewife and always used to look forward to do something never done before by any woman. Her dazzling office in Greater Kailash in New Delhi appraises the visitor of her confident personality.

While studying cosmetic chemistry from abroad, she explored into age–old Indian Ayurbedic system of herbs through which she could research, discover and develop herbal care and medicines, exploiting the herbal market commercially. Heavily pricing her product, she launched her one–room shop with a meager investment of Rs 3500. People rushed to buy her facial cream which was exorbitant as composed to a similar product already available in the next market. She personally used to fly to different cities of the country and lectured and publicized Ayurveda. Her marketing strategy was a unique one perusing more clients than she could handle.

Today, her products are being exported to over 130 countries and she attributes her success to her determination. Completing more than two and a half decades in this business, she is expanding her empire quoting that that 'failure' word does not exist in her dictionary and she never stops trying. Quoting Shahnaz Husain, "In life you get what you negotiate. Any woman has the capacity to do what I did–it does not matter what you want, what matters is how badly you do it."

REFRENCES

1. Holt, David H. Entrepreneurship-New Venture Creation, Prentice Hall of India Private Limited, New Delhi, 1998.
2. Lalitha Iyer: Women Entrepreneurs—Challenges And Strategies Frederic Exert Sifting (FES), New Delhi, 1991.
3. M.Soundarapandian: Women Entrepreneurship—Issues and Strategies. Edited Volume. Kanishka Publishers, New Delhi, 1999.
4. Pattanaik, Swadeep R and Patnaik, Umesh C, business Environment and Entrepreneurship, Dhanpat Rai & Sons, Delhi, 2nd Revised Edition, 1994.
5. S.S.Khanka: Entrepreneurial Development S.Chand & Co. New Delhi, 1999.
6. Swarajaya Lakshmi, C., Development of Women Entrepreneurship in India-Problems and Prospectus, Discovery Publishing House, New Delhi.
7. Uddin, Sami, Entrepreneurship Development in India, Mittal Publications, Delhi, 1st Edition, 1989.
8. Wadhwa, Raj K. Davar, Jimmy and Rao P. Bhaskara, Entrepreneur and Enterprise Management, Kanishka Publishers, Distributers. New Delhi, 1st Edition, 1998.

4

Promotional Institution, Association and Government Agencies of the Development of Women Entrepreneurs

Prof. H.D.Barad

ABSTRACT

There is a realization that full involvement of women in industrial development would ensure effective utilization of available labour and improve quality of life. This leads to state that action must be taken by the government to analyze current status and potential role of women in the process of industrialization with a view to bring positive change which would result in sharing of responsibilities and benefits by both sexes. Effective and adequate legislation for social facilities, health provision, and maternity and social security benefits might enhance the process of women's involvement in the development process.

Several Institutions, Government agencies and Association are operating at national and regional level for the promote self employment, participation of women in rural industries, development of appropriate technology, role of consultancy and role of financial institutions. Women entrepreneurship gained much importance in the India. Many states have come up with several schemes that seek to promote the entrepreneurial skills of women's unemployment and poverty in India can be tackled efficiently by developing entrepreneurship in them. In India, the role of association belonging to trade, professionals and industries had been largely confined in marking representations in the decision making machineries of the central and state government. With a growth of entrepreneurial wave in the country a many associations of women entrepreneurs have emerged extend a helping hand and creating a congenial environment for the broadening the base for widespread entrepreneurship in rural and urban areas. On the review of the functions of various association/ institutions listed, it was observed that same government development agencies and institutions have made serious attempts to undertake the task of entrepreneurial promotion. The various financial/technical institutions and organizations and the different departments of the Central and State governments engaged in entrepreneurship development should establish a greater degree of co-operation, Liaison closer working relationship and better understanding. No tangible result can, therefore, be expected unless all the agencies involved in the task of entrepreneurship development work with determination. Zeal and a sense of dedication and commitment.

INTRODUCTION

Today, several associations, institutions and government agencies are operating at national and regional level for the promotion of women entrepreneurs. Here, an attempt is made to discuss the role of the importance associations, institutions and Goverment agencies in entrepreneurship development, their activities, schemes and programmers undertaken to improve entrepreneurship.

Small-scale sector in India over the past 55 years has made significant contributions towards building a strong national economy. The government has also started taking initiatives by providing various types of incentives and subsidies to the small-scale industries for improving their economic condition and also providing employment, thereby increasing the standard of living the rural masses. The women in the rural sector have immense potential and expertise in art and craft, handloom, food products like papad, pickles, spices, clay utensils, bamboo baskets etc. Small scale units create more self-employment opportunities with less capital investment requirements, the raw materials are locally based and there is less environmental pollution. Small firms require simple technology and law managerial skills. Export promotion of product developed by small-scale industries help to earn valuable foreign exchange and preserve the balance of payment status. There were more than 295682 women entrepreneurs in India during 1995-96.

INSTITUTIONAL FRAMEWORK FOR SMALL—SCALE INDUSTRIES IN INDIA

Keeping in view the importance of entrepreneurs of Small—scale Industry, the government of India has made considerable efforts to promote its growth during the last five decades. The strategy for its development comprises formulation and pursuance of deliberate policies for its protection and development, stepping up plan allocations, evolving and implementing various programmes for its development including extension of confessionals finance, both short-term and long term, through a plethora of supporting institutions. The following is the institutional framework for small-scale industries in India.

Institutional Framework for Small-scale Industries in India

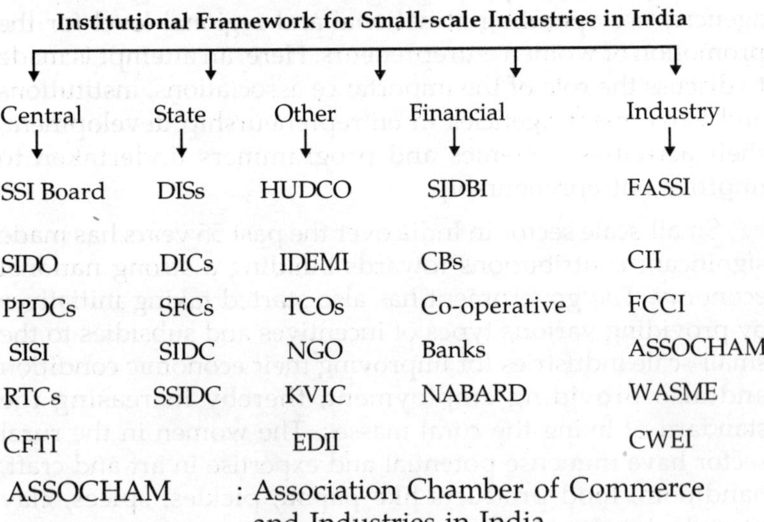

ASSOCHAM : Association Chamber of Commerce and Industries in India

CBs : Commercial Banks

CFIT : Central Footwear Testing Institute

CII	: Confederation of Indian Industries
CWEL	: Consortium of Women Entrepreneurs in India
DIs	: District Industries
DICs	: District Industries Centre
EDII	: Entrepreneurship Development Institute of India
FICCI	: Federation of Indian Chamber of Commerce and Industries
HUDCO	: Housing and Urban Development Corporation
IDEMI	: Institute for Design and Electrical Measuring
KVIC	: Khadi and Village Industries Commission
NABARD	: National Bank of Agriculture and Rural Development
NGO	: Non Government Organisation
NISIET	: National Institute of Small Industries Extension and Training
NSIC Ltd	: National Small Industries Corporation Limited
NIESBUD	: National Institute for Entrepreneurship and Small Business Development.
SSI Board	: Small-scale Industries Board
SIDO	: Small-scale Industries Development Organisation
PPDCs	: Product-cum-Process Development Centres
SISI	: Small Industries Service Institute
SFCs	: State Finance Corporations
SDBI	: Small Industrial Bank of India
SSIDC	: State Small Industries Development Corporation

RTCs : Regional Training Centres

TCOS : Technical Consultancy Organisation

WASME : World Association of Small and Medium Entreprises

CENTRAL GOVERNMENT INSTITUTIONS

Small Industries Development Organisation (SIDO)

This is an apex body and nodal agency for formulating, co-ordinating and monitoring the policies and programmes for promotion and development of small scale industries. It provides a comprehensive range of facilities and service including consultancy it techno-economic managerial aspects, training, common facility services, common processing and training, common facility services, common processing and facilities, cooing facilities, marketing assistance etc. to small scale units. All these services are provided through its network of 25 small industries services Institutes, 20 branch SISIs, 41 extension centers, 4 regional testing centers one product and process development centre, 3 footwear training centers and 5 production centers.

Small Industries Development Bank of India (SIDBI)

SIDBI was set up by an Act of Parliament, as an apex institution for promotion, financing and development of industries in small scale sector and for coordinating the functions of other institutions engaged in similar activities. It commenced operations on April 2, 1990. SIDBI extends direct/ indirect financial assistance to SSIs, assisting the entire spectrum of small and tiny sector industries on All India basis.

The range of assistance comprising financing, extension support and promotional, are made available through appropriate schemes of direct and indirect assistance for the following purposes:

Setting up of new projects

- Expansion, diversification, modernisation, technology up gradation, quality improvement, rehabilitation of existing units

- Strengthening of marketing capabilities of SSI units
- Development of infrastructure for SSIs and
- Export promotion

Direct Assistance Schemes

SIDBI directly assists SSIs under Project Finance Scheme, Equipment Finance Scheme, Marketing Scheme, Vendor Development Scheme, Infrastructural Development Scheme, ISO-9000, Technology Development and Modernisation Fund, Venture Capital Scheme, assistance for leasing to NBFCs, SFCs and resource support to institutions in involved in the development and financing of small scale sector. This schemes are mainly targeted at addressing some of the major problems of SSIs in areas such as high project, marketing infrastructural development, delayed realization of bills, obsolescence of technology, quality improvement, export financing and venture capital assistance.

Indirect Assistance Schemes

Under its indirect schemes, SIDBI extends refinance of loans to small sector by primary Leading Institutions (PLIs) Vis SFCs, SIDCs and Banks. At present, such refinance assistance is extended to 892 PLIs and these PLIs extend credit through a net work of more than 65000 branches all over the country. All the scheme of SIDBI both direct and indirect assistance are in operation in all the States of the country through 39 regional/branch offices of SIDBI.

Promotional and Development Activities

SIDBI is actively involved in promoting tiny and small scale industries by means of its promotional and development activities through suitable professional agencies for organizing Entrepreneurship Development, Technological Upgradation and Mordernisation Programmes. Micro credit Schemes and assistance under Mahila Vicas Nithi to bring about economic development of women specially the rural poor by providing them avenues for training and employment opportunities.

A.	Refinance against term lons in respect of projects/activities eseligible for assistance under the Scheme	Interest on term loans for fixed assets and working capital advance (exculding interest tax) (% p.a)	Interest on Refinance (% p.a.)
(i)	Upto and inclusive of ₹25,000	12.0	9.0
(ii)	Over ₹25,000 and upto ₹2 lakh	Not exceeding 13.5	10.5
B.	Refinance against term loans in respect of projects/activitie eligible for assistance under TDMF and ISO 9000 Schemes (Applicable to all eligible institutions) (except RRBs)	Interest on term loans (excluding interest tax) (% p.a.)	Interest on Refinance (% p.a.)
(i)	Upto and inclusive of ₹25,000	12.0	9.0
(ii)	Over ₹25,000 and up to ₹2 lakh	Not exceeding 13.5	10.5
(iii)	Over ₹2 lakh	Not exceeding 14.0	12.0

Industrial Development Bank of India (IDBI)

Scheme for Women Entrepreneurs: The scheme has been formulated with the twin objective of:

- Providing training and extension services support to women entrepreneurs through a comprehensive package suited to their skills and socio-economic status; and
- Extending financial assistance on concessional terms, to enable them to set up industrial units in the small-scale sector.

  Under this scheme, programmes for training and extension services for women entrepreneurs are organized by IDBI through designated/approved agencies independently, and /or in association with other development agencies like the Entrepreneurship Development Institute of India, Technical Consultancy Organisation, Central/state social Welfare Boards and KVIC.

Mahila Vicas Nithi (MVN) scheme: Recognizing the role of voluntary agencies in improving the socio-economic status of women, IDBI decided to set up a special development fund (Mahila Vikas Nithi) with an initial allocation of Rs. 33 crores from its Technical Assistance Fund. Assistance by way of grant and soft loans is to be made available from the Nidhi. Registered voluntary organization which have a proven track record, well functioning governing body, and working exclusively for women's development, are eligible for assistance.

Activities which could be supported under this scheme include setting up training-cum development centers, undertaking up gradation programs, marketing assistance, management up gradation, and other such industrial activities which improve the economic status of women assistance under the scheme is towards one-time capital expenditure, since it is expected that recurring expenses of voluntary agencies can be met out of other sources of funding.

Scheme for Re-finance Assistance to Women Entrepreneurs: All projects in the SSI Sector (including cottage, village and tiny industries) Promoted and managed by women entrepreneurs are eligible for assistance under this scheme. The minimum promoter's contribution has to be 12.5 of the project cost for units set up in category 'A' backward district, and 15% of the project cost in all others cases, irrespective of location.

The expected debt-equity ratio 3:1. The rate of interest is 9% of the annum on IDBI re-finance with the corresponding rate on the loans of the primary lenders not to exceed 12.5 per cent per annum. The loan is repayable over a period not exceeding 10 years, including a moratorium of 2 years.

Re-finance is provided to the extent of 100 per cent of the loan to SFCs/SIDCs, if covered under ARS, and 85 per cent if the proposals come under NRS. However, for projected set up in 'A' category backward district, the extent of re-finance will be 90 per cent in the case of banks, re-finance could be upto 75 per cent of the loan amount, both under ARS and NRS.

Primary lenders may stipulate such security for the loan as they may deem appropriate. However, no collateral security need be obtain

Industrial Finance Corporation of India (IFCI)

Interest Subsidy for Women Entrepreneurs: The main object of this scheme is to provide incentive to women having business acumen and entrepreneurial traits, so that avenues of self-development and self-employment are created for them and they can contribute to the industrial development of the country.

Subject to eligibility criteria, all industrial project whether in the rural, cottage, tiny or small scale (including ancillary) sectors (with a project cost up to Rs. 10 lakhs), if set up by a women entrepreneur on the town with a minimum financial stake of 51 per cent in the unit, will be covered under the scheme. The scheme is operated through the State Financial Corporations (SFCs/State-level financial institutions performing the role of SFCs/banks) granting assistance to women entrepreneurs.

To be eligible for availing the subsidy under the scheme, a women entrepreneur is required to fulfill set specified criteria.

The disbursement of the subsidy is made by IFCI upon receiving an application for interest subsidy under the scheme from the women entrepreneur concerned with due recommendations and certificates from the SFC/Bank, as may be required. The actual disbursement of the subsidy is made off the interest on the amount granted to the unit.

Public Sector Banks

(A) Dena Bank

This bank has special schemes to finance women entrepreneurs. Some incentives offered are 5 per cent concession in the interest rate, no processing fee, easy payment option and no penalty for repayment. The loan amount is up to 5 lakhs for women entrepreneurs who are professionals. The loan is also extended to artists, small and medium cottage industries run by women.

(B) State Bank of India: *Name of the loan: Stree Shakti Package*

This is special offer of loans to women entrepreneurs. It gives concession in promoter's margin and rate of interest. The aim of the scheme is to inspire women to start new venture. No secturity is needed for loans up to 5 laks for industrial units.

(C) Bank of India: *Name of the loan: Priyadarshini*

This is facility offered to women to set up small, Village and cottage industries. The loan covers the payment for machinery. There is a one per cent cut in the interest rate for loan above 2 lakhs.

(D) Canara Bank: *Name of the loan Can Mahila*

This is a loan meet the financing needs of women, who may be housewives, working women or self-employed women. It can be used to buy household articles, gold, jewelers computers etc. Women between the ages of 18 to 55 can avail this loan. For the salaried and self employed as well as for women with a family of 1.5 lakhs, the loan limit is 50,000 INR.

(E) Union Bank of India: *Name of the loan: Vikalang Mahila Vikas Yojana*

This is a special scheme for handicapped women for starting their own ventures. Physically handicapped women are identified and after providing vocational training according to their aptitude, financial assistance of 25000 is offered to start the new venture.

(F) UCO Bank: *Name of the loan Nari Shakti*

This scheme is to provide financial assistance to salaried women. Concession is offered on interest and repayment is in 5 years in equated installments.

(G) Central Bank of India: *Name of loan: Kalyani*

This scheme is specially introduced to offer financial assistance to Women Entrepreneurs for economic pursuits in industry, Agricultural and Allied Activities, Business or profession. The Bank with a network of branches spread throughout the country welcomes women entrepreneurs to avail financial assistance for pursuing vocations of their choice.

Small Business: For entrepreneurs who intend to provide services such as a small lunch home/canteen, mobile restaurant, circulating library etc.

Professional and Self-Employed: Entrepreneurs who are specially qualified/skilled and experienced like Doctors, Chatered Accountants, Engineers or trained in Art or Craft etc.

Retail Trade: For entrepreneurs who intend to engage in retail trading of various commodities.

Village and Cottage/ Tiny Industries: For entrepreneurs who are engaged in manufacturing, processing, preservation and services such as Handloom, Weaving Handicraft, Food-processing, Garment marketing etc. In village and small towns with a population not exceeding 50,000/- utilizing locally available resources/skills.

Small Scale Industries: To start a unit engaged in manufacture, processing or preservation of goods.

Agriculture and Allied Activities: For women entrepreneurs who are engaged in agricultural and allied activities, such as rising of crops, floriculture, fisheries, bookeeping, nursery, sericulture etc. and also trading in agricultural products.

Government Sponsored Programmes: Apart from the above schemes, women entrepreneurs are also financed under the various Government Sponsored Programmes where capital subsidies are available.

Others terms and conditions for the above facilities under Cent Kalyani i.e. quantum of loan, margin, interest, repayment, documentation etc. are as applicable under their respective schemes.

(H) Oriental Bank of Commerce: *Name of the loan: Mahila Vikas Yojana*

In this special scheme for the benefit of women entrepreneurs, the loan amount offered is between 2 and 10 lakhs, with a 2 per cent concession in interest. Loan above 10 lakhs are also offered at 1 per cent concession. Enterprise consisting of all units managed by women and where they have a share of 51 per cent are eligible for thios loan. In case of term loan, the repayment period up to seven years with a maximum grace period of 12 months depending on the nature of the activity.

(I) ICICI Bank: *Name of the Loan: Women's Account*

This is a scheme formulated by the new generation bank for women. Under the scheme any women, with any relative an account in the bank can open an account without any documentation.

NATIONAL LEVEL TRAINING INSTITUTIONS

1 Entrepreneurship Development Institute of India (EDII)

EDII was established in March, 1983 at Ahmedabad as a resource organization at the national level. It is not a profit organization. It is an autonomous body. EDII is sponsored by the apex financial institutions, the IDBI, ICICI, IFCI and SBI.

EDII is a national resource institution committed to entrepreneurship education and research, striving to provide innovative training techniques, competent faculty support, teaching and training material, besides sharing benefits of in house research as well as experience in relevant sphere. EDII has spreading entrepreneurship movements throughout the country. EDII has linkages with a nation-wide network of organisatins and institutions committed entrepreneurship development. It is an inter-regional centre for entrepreneurship and investment training sponsored by United Nations Industrial Development Organisation and Government of India.

EDII organizes conferences, workshops, seminars for interaction between Non-Government Organization and bankers to facilitate creation and development of business enterprise. The institute has taken several research initiatives in the area of industrial environment, industrial clusters policy and support system and has designed programmes to sensitive the environment to provide extensive support to potential existing entrepreneurs.

Beside the above varied programmes the institute the has an innovative centre sponsored by National Science and Technology Entrepreneurship Development

2 National Institute for Entrepreneurship and Small Business Development (NIESBUD)

The National Institute for Entrepreneurship and Small Businesses Development is an apex body established by the Ministry of Industry, Government of India, for co-coordinating and overseeing the activities of various institutions/ agencies engaged in entrepreneurial development in small industry and small business.

Besides its many activities in promoting entrepreneurship in the country, NIESBUD has evolved model syllabi for conducting EDPs for various client including women. A syllabus for developing rural women as entrepreneurs was also designed by the Institute as per the recommendations of the National Level Standing Committee on Women Entrepreneurs. NIESBUD also organized national and international training programs exclusively for potential women entrepreneurs and women trainers/promoters in the area of entrepreneurship development. It also undertakes exploratory research in the field of women's entrepreneurship.

3 International Centre for Entrepreneurship and Development (ICECD), Ahmedabad.

ICECD is an autonomous organization established by a group of professionals to promote women entrepreneurs through training, educational and research initiatives at both the national and international level. Some of the areas that

ICECD works in include gender issues, women's economic empowerment, management capability building in government and non-government organizations, awareness generation for enterprise establishment, delivery and support, and technology identification and transfer. ICECD has had experience in development a large number of women for economic self-sufficiency in rural and urban areas of many development countries. Based in its experience it has also developed a few training manuals such as Group Entrepreneurship for Rural Women and Trainers' Manual.

NATIONAL LEVEL WOMEN ENTREPRENEURS ASSOCIATION AND ORGANISATION.

1 National Alliance of Young Entrepreneurs (NAYE)

NAYE is the leading organization in India who organizes international conferences in India as abroad. It promotes women entrepreneurs to participate actively in the work of economic development. NAYE seeks to strengthen forces of unity among women entrepreneurs. This Association continuously urging the central and state Governments to provide special facilities and incentives for women entrepreneurs.

The association is constantly fighting for liberal help from the government so as to effectively participate in rural and urban development programme based on entrepreneurship.

NAYE has set up a women's wing in 1975 which assists women entrepreneurs in the following manner:

- Organising seminar, workshops and training programmes.
- Development of management and production capabilities.
- Identifying investment opportunities.
- Sponsoring exhibitions, delegations, participation in trade fairs, buyer-seller specialized conferences etc.
- Getting better access to capital, infrastructure and markets etc.

2 Federation of Indian Chambers of Commerce and Industry (FICCI Ladies Organisation)

FICCI is the oldest and the strongest association of business, commencing operations in India in 1928. FICCI has a separate women's cell which held its first Entrepreneurship Development Programme for women in 1986.It has also organized several training courses specifically for women entrepreneurs, under the ILO's improve your Business (IYB) programme.

3 National Small Industries Corporation (NSIC).

The National Small Industries Corporation (NSIC) was set up by the Government of India in 1955 to promote and develop small scale industries in the country.

In the process, it extends help in the establishment of new, small and ancillary industries and in the modernisation of existing ones by supplying

4 Indian Council for Women Entrepreneurs

It is situated in New Delhi and is rendering valuable services for the promotion for women for women entrepreneurship country.

CONCLUSION

On the review of the functions of various association/ institutions listed above, it was observed that the some government development agencies and institutions have made serious attempts to undertake the task of entrepreneurial promotion. The various financial/technical institutions and organizations and the different departments of the Central and State governments engaged in entrepreneurship development should establish a greater degree of co-operation, Liaison closer working relationship and better understanding. No tangible result can, therefore, be expected unless all the agencies involved in the task of entrepreneurship development work with determination. Zeal and a sense of dedication and commitment.

REFERENCES

I Books

1. C. Swarajyalakshmi "Development of Women Entrepreneurship in India—Problem and Prospect" Discovery Publishing House, New Delhi.
2. Dr. Gokul P. Kapase. "Development of Women Entrepreneurship in India" Shubham Publication, Kanpur.
3. K. Sudarsan Himachalam Dasaraju "Financing Micro, Small and Medium Enterprises" The Association Publishers Dhulkot.
4. G. K. Patra, P .C. Misra and G.S Lall. "Financing Small Scale Industry" Discovery Publishing House, New Delhi.
5. Syed Vazith Hussain. "*Small Scale Industries in the New Millennium*" Srup & Sons.
6. M.Laxmi Narasaiah, N. Annuradha. "*Growth and Performance of Small Scale Industry*" Discovery Publishing House, New Delhi.
7. Vasant Desai, Third Ed. "*Small-scale Industries and Entrepreneurship*" Himalaya Publication House

II Websites

- http://www.junagadh.Gujarat.gov.in
- http://www.bankofindia.com
- http://www.msmes gov.in
- http://www.lgu-udyog.com
- http://www.bulletin.rbi.org.in
- http://www.vijayabank.com
- http://www.ucobank.com
- http://www.statebankofindia.com
- http://www.obcindia.com.in

5

Women Entrepreneurs in India

Prof. A.K.Panda

ABSTRACT

Women in business are a recent phenomenon in India. By and large they had confide themselves to petty business and tiny cottage industries. Women entrepreneurs engaged in business due to push and pull factors. Which encourage women to have an independent occupation and stands on their own legs. A sense towards independent decision-making on their life and career is the motivational factor behind this urge. Saddled with household chores and domestic responsibilities women want to get independence. Under the influence of these factors the women entrepreneurs choose a profession as a challenge and as an urge to do something new. Such situation is described as pull factors. While in push factors women engaged in business activities due to family compulsion and the responsibility is thrust upon them.

Key words: entrepreneurship, self motivation, socio-cultural, market, oriented, pull factors, UNIDO.

INTRODUCTION

The principle of gender equality is enshrined in the Indian Constitution in its Preamble, Fundamental Rights, Fundamental Duties and Directive Principles. The Constitution not only grants equality to women, but also empowers the

State to adopt measures of positive discrimination in favor of women. Empowerment is the one of the key factors in determining the success of development is the status and position of women in the society. We put a special focus on empowering women and girls, because we believe they hold the key to long-lasting social change in communities. Empowering women must be a united approach, a cause that requires continued attention and stewardship by all. We need to augment our efforts for empowering women and enhance their progress. It is our moral, social and constitutional responsibility to ensure their progress by providing them with equal rights and opportunities. Today women with their smartness, grace and elegance have conquered the whole world. They with their hard work and sincerity have excelled in each and every profession. Women are considered to be more honest, meticulous, and efficient and hence more and more companies prefer hiring women for better performance and result.

ENTREPRENEURS, WOMEN

The Indian sociological set up has been traditionally a male dominated. Women are considered as weaker sex and always to depend on men folk in their family and outside, throughout their life. They are left with lesser commitments and kept as a dormant force for a quite long time. The Indian culture made them only subordinates and executors of the decisions made by other male members ,in the basic family structure. The traditional set up is changing in the modern era. The transformation of social fabric of the Indian society, in terms of increased educational status of women and varied aspirations for better living, necessitated a change in the life style of Indian women. Indian families do have the privilege of being envied by the westerners, since women here are taking more responsibilities in bringing up children and maintaining a better home with love and affection. At the family level, the task of coordinating various activities in a much effective manner, without feeling the pinch of inconveniences, is being carried out by the women folk. Thus, the Indian women have basic characters in themselves in the present sociological and cultural set up as follows.

That Indian women are considered as Sakthi, which means source of power. Effectively coordinating the available factors and resources. Efficient execution of decisions imposed on them Clear vision and ambition on the improvement of family and children. Patience and bearing the sufferings on behalf of others and Ability to work physically more at any age. For a country whose population of women alone is more than the total population of many other countries, we are pretty low where their treatment is concerned. The number of sexual abuse and domestic violence cases against women clearly throws light on the fact that women in India do not enjoy even basic rights; their health, education and empowerment unfortunately take a back seat under such a scenario. The least we can do is give half our population an equal world.

WOMEN'S STRONG DESIRE TO DO SOMETHING

'Women' as an entrepreneur in India: women are companies are fast-growing economies in almost all countries. The latent entrepreneurial potential of women have changed little by little by the growing awareness of the role and status of economic society. Skills, knowledge and adaptability of the economy led to a major reason for women in business. 'Women Entrepreneurs' is a person who denies the role of their personal needs to participate and be accepted economically independent. Strong desire to do something positive, is a high-quality women entrepreneurs who contribute to the position values of family and social life. The advent of media, women are aware of their own characteristics, rights and work situations. The glass ceilings are broken and women are engaged in the industry for power pappad. The challenges and opportunities for women in the digital age are growing, as job seekers turn to job creation. They are growing as a designer, interior designers, exporters, publishing, clothing, and always looking for new modes of economic participation.

In India, although women constitute the majority of the total population, the business world still composed primarily of men. Women in advanced countries are recognized and its reputation in the business world. But Indian women face as entrepreneurs are important boundary conditions as:*(a) Lack of confidence*—in general, women lack confidence in their strength and skill. The members of the family and society are reluctant to stand beside their growth. To some extent this situation in Indian women and even change a profound change with the growth of entrepreneurship erhöhen;*(b) The socio-cultural barriers;* women in the family and personal obligations are sometimes a major obstacle to successful careers in business. Few women are able to manage both home and business efficiently devote sufficient time for all of their priority tasks durchzuführen;*(c) market risks:* a stiff competition in the market and lack mobility of the dependence of women and women entrepreneurs essential intermediary. Many business women struggling to gain market and its products popular. So you are not fully aware of changing market conditions and therefore cannot make effective use of media and internet;*(d) motivators:* Self-motivation can be achieved by a mindset for a successful business, attitude to risk and attitude towards the society by economic, social responsibility to assume.

Other factors are likely to support families, government policies, financial support from public and private institutions, and the environment for women to start businesses schaffen;*(e) knowledge of business administration:* women need to stay on the skills and knowledge to acquire all the functional areas of business management training. This can help women excel in decision making and further developing a good business netzwerk;*(f) Awareness of financial aid:* Various institutions in the financial sector, their maximum support in the form of incentives the loans can, systems, etc. Even in this case not all women entrepreneurs to be aware of any institutional support. Thus, the sincere efforts entrepreneurs cannot reach entrepreneurs in rural and backward region;*(g) programs for training presentations*—Training programmes and workshops for all types of entrepreneurs through social organizations and well be available, depending on the time, skills and subject training. These programs are very helpful for new, rural entrepreneurs and youth, creating unity of small and medium enterprises on their own möchten;*(h) identify resources available*—Women are reluctant to find access to their needs in the areas of finance and marketing of justice.

Despite the growth of fungi associations, institutions and government regulations, women are not entrepreneurial and dynamically optimize the resources as reserves, women's assets or business Freiwilligen.But humanity trained and technically and professionally trained to manage their own business, but be encouraged as a dependent on the points of employment. The talent to discover young women identified to be trained and used for various industries to increase productivity in the industrial sector. An enabling environment for all women are needed to better communicate and involve strong corporate values in business. The additional business opportunities, the approach recently for the women entrepreneurs are: • Environment Friendly Bio-computing technology to enable companies • Event Management • Tourism telecommunications industry Plastics • Vermiculture • Mineral water • Sericulture • Herbs and flowers of healthy food, fruits and vegetables empowerment of women entrepreneurs is to achieve sustainable development objectives and constraints hampering their growth must be eradicated essential to ensure the full participation will enable the company . In addition to training programmes, newsletters, mentoring, fairs and exhibitions can also be a source of entrepreneurship development. Consequently, the results of the company has achieved rapid and find more profitable business opportunities. Therefore, the promotion of entrepreneurship among women is probably a shortcut to economic growth and rapid development. Let us try to eliminate all forms of sex discrimination and thus enable 'women' in a contractor to equality with men.

MAJOR CONSTRAINTS

Women owned businesses are highly increasing in the economies of almost all countries. The hidden entrepreneurial potentials of women have gradually been changing with the growing sensitivity to the role and economic status in the society. Skill, knowledge and adaptability in business are the main reasons for women to emerge into business ventures.' Women Entrepreneur' is a person who accepts challenging role to meet her personal needs and become economically independent. A strong desire to do something positive is an inbuilt quality of entrepreneurial women, who is capable of contributing values in both family and social life. With the advent of media, women are aware of their own traits, rights and also the work situations. The glass ceilings are shattered and women are found indulged in every line of business from pappad to power cables. The challenges and opportunities provided to the women of digital era are growing rapidly that the job seekers are turning into job creators. They are flourishing as designers, interior decorators, exporters, publishers, garment manufacturers and still exploring new avenues of economic participation. In India, although women constitute the majority of the total population, the entrepreneurial world is still a male dominated one. Women in advanced nations are recognized and are more prominent in the business world. But the Indian women entrepreneurs are facing some major constraints like:

a) *Lack of confidence:* In general, women lack confidence in their strength and competence. The family members and the society are reluctant to stand beside their entrepreneurial growth. To a certain extent, this situation is changing among Indian women and yet to face a tremendous change to increase the rate of growth in entrepreneurship.

b) *Socio-cultural barriers:* Women's family and personal obligations are sometimes a great barrier for succeeding in business career. Only few women are able to manage both home and business efficiently, devoting enough time to perform all their responsibilities in priority.

c) *Market-oriented risks:* Stiff competition in the market and lack of mobility of women make the dependence of women entrepreneurs on middleman indispensable. Many business women find it difficult to capture the market and make their products popular. They are not fully aware of the changing market conditions and hence can effectively utilize the services of media and internet.

d) *Motivational factors:* Self motivation can be realized through a mind set for a successful business, attitude to take up risk and behavior towards the business society by shouldering the social responsibilities. Other factors are family support, Government policies, financial assistance from public and private institutions and also the environment suitable for women to establish business units.

e) *Knowledge in Business Administration:* Women must be educated and trained constantly to acquire the skills and knowledge in all the functional areas of business management. This can facilitate women to excel in decision making process and develop a good business network.

f) *Awareness about the financial assistance:* Various institutions in the financial sector extend their maximum support in the form of incentives, loans, schemes etc. Even then every woman entrepreneur may not be aware of all the assistance provided by the institutions. So the sincere efforts taken towards women entrepreneurs may not reach the entrepreneurs in rural and backward areas.

g) *Exposed to the training programmes:* Training programs and workshops for every type of entrepreneur is available through the social and welfare associations, based on duration, skill and the purpose of the training program. Such programs are really useful to new, rural and young entrepreneurs who want to set up a small and medium scale unit on their own.

h) *Identifying the available resources:* Women are hesitant to find out the access to cater their needs in the financial and marketing areas. In spite of the mushrooming growth of associations, institutions, and the schemes from the government side, women are not enterprising and dynamic to optimize the resources in the form of reserves, assets mankind or business volunteers.

Highly educated, technically sound and professionally qualified women should be encouraged for managing their own business, rather than dependent on wage employment outlets. The unexplored talents of young women can be identified, trained and used for various types of industries to increase the productivity in the industrial sector. A desirable environment is necessary for every woman to inculcate entrepreneurial values and involve greatly in business dealings.

Empowering women entrepreneurs is essential for achieving the goals of sustainable development and the bottlenecks hindering their growth must be eradicated to entitle full participation in the business. Apart from training programmes, Newsletters, mentoring, trade fairs and exhibitions also can be a source for entrepreneurial development. As a result, the desired outcomes of the business are quickly achieved and more of remunerative business opportunities are found. Henceforth, promoting entrepreneurship among women is certainly a short-cut to rapid economic growth and development. Let us try to eliminate all forms of gender discrimination and thus allow 'women' to be an entrepreneur at par with men .

PROBLEMS

Women in India are faced many problems to get ahead their life in business. A few problems can be detailed as:

1. The greatest deterrent to women entrepreneurs is that they are women. A kind of patriarchal male dominant social order is the building block to them in their way towards business success. Male members think it a big risk financing the ventures run by women.

2. The financial institutions are skeptical about the entrepreneurial abilities of women. The bankers consider women loonies as higher risk than men loonies. The bankers put unrealistic and unreasonable securities to get loan to women entrepreneurs. According to a report by the United Nations Industrial Development Organization

(UNIDO), "despite evidence that women's loan repayment rates are higher than men's, women still face more difficulties in obtaining credit," often due to discriminatory attitudes of banks and informal lending groups (UNIDO, 1995b).

3. Entrepreneurs usually require financial assistance of some kind to launch their ventures—be it a formal bank loan or money from a savings account. Women in developing nations have little access to funds, due to the fact that they are concentrated in poor rural communities with few opportunities to borrow money (Starcher, 1996; UNIDO, 1995a). The women entrepreneurs are suffering from inadequate financial resources and working capital. The women entrepreneurs lack access to external funds due to their inability to provide tangible security. Very few women have the tangible property in hand.
4. Women's family obligations also bar them from becoming successful entrepreneurs in both developed and developing nations. "Having primary responsibility for children, home and older dependent family members, few women can devote all their time and energies to their business" (Starcher, 1996, p. 8).The financial institutions discourage women entrepreneurs on the belief that they can at any time leave their business and become housewives again. The result is that they are forced to rely on their own savings, and loan from relatives and family friends.
5. Indian women give more emphasis to family ties and relationships. Married women have to make a fine balance between business and home. More over the business success is depends on the support the family members extended to women in the business process and management. The interest of the family members is a determinant factor in the realization of women folk business aspirations.
6. Another argument is that women entrepreneurs have low-level management skills. They have to depend on office

staffs and intermediaries, to get things done, especially, the marketing and sales side of business. Here there is more probability for business fallacies like the intermediaries take major part of the surplus or profit. Marketing means mobility and confidence in dealing with the external world, both of which women have been discouraged from developing by social conditioning. Even when they are otherwise in control of an enterprise, they often depend on males of the family in this area.

7. The male-female competition is another factor, which develop hurdles to women entrepreneurs in the business management process. Despite the fact that women entrepreneurs are good in keeping their service prompt and delivery in time, due to lack of organizational skills compared to male entrepreneurs women have to face constraints from competition. The confidence to travel across day and night and even different regions and states are less found in women compared to male entrepreneurs. This shows the low level freedom of expression and freedom of mobility of the women entrepreneurs.

8. Knowledge of alternative source of raw materials availability and high negotiation skills are the basic requirement to run a business. Getting the raw materials from different souse with discount prices is the factor that determines the profit margin. Lack of knowledge of availability of the raw materials and low-level negotiation and bargaining skills are the factors, which affect women entrepreneur's business adventures.

9. Knowledge of latest technological changes, know-how, and education level of the person are significant factor that affect business. The literacy rate of women in India is found at low level compared to male population. Many women in developing nations lack the education needed to spur successful entrepreneurship. They are ignorant of new technologies or unskilled in their use, and often unable to do research and gain the necessary training (UNIDO, 1995b, p.1). Although great advances are being made in

technology, many women's illiteracy, strucutural difficulties, and lack of access to technical training prevent the technology from being beneficial or even available to females ("Women Entrepreneurs in Poorest Countries," 2001). According to The Economist, this lack of knowledge and the continuing treatment of women as second-class citizens keeps them in a pervasive cycle of poverty ("The Female Poverty Trap," 2001). The studies indicates that uneducated women donot have the knowledge of measurement and basic accounting.

10. Low-level risk taking attitude is another factor affecting women folk decision to get into business. Low-level education provides low-level self-confidence and self-reliance to the women-folk to engage in business, which is continuous risk taking and strategic decision making profession. Investing money, maintaining the operations and ploughing back money for surplus generation requires high risk taking attitude, courage and confidence. Though the risk tolerance ability of the women folk in day-to-day life is high compared to male members, while in business it is found opposite to that.
11. Achievement motivation of the women folk found less compared to male members. The low level of education and confidence leads to low level achievement and advancement motivation among women folk to engage in business operations and running a business concern.
12. Finally high production cost of some business operations adversely affects the development of women entrepreneurs. The installation of new machineries during expansion of the productive capacity and like similar factors dissuades the women entrepreneurs from venturing into new areas.

HOW TO DEVELOP WOMEN ENTREPRENEURS?

Right efforts on from all areas are required in the development of women entrepreneurs and their greater participation in the entrepreneurial activities. Following efforts can be taken into account for effective development of women entrepreneurs:

- Consider women as specific target group for all developmental programmes.
- Better educational facilities and schemes should be extended to women folk from government part.
- Adequate training programme on management skills to be provided to women community.
- Encourage women's participation in decision-making.
- Vocational training to be extended to women community that enables them to understand the production process and production management.
- Skill development to be done in women's polytechnics and industrial training institutes. Skills are put to work in training-cum-production workshops.
- Training on professional competence and leadership skill to be extended to women entrepreneurs.
- Training and counselling on a large scale of existing women entrepreneurs to remove psychological causes like lack of self-confidence and fear of success.
- Counselling through the aid of committed NGOs, psychologists, managerial experts and technical personnel should be provided to existing and emerging women entrepreneurs.
- Continuous monitoring and improvement of training programmes.
- Activities in which women are trained should focus on their marketability and profitability.
- Making provision of marketing and sales assistance from government part.
- To encourage more passive women entrepreneurs the Women training programme should be organised that taught to recognize her own psychological needs and express them.
- State finance corporations and financing institutions should

permit by statute to extend purely trade related finance to women entrepreneurs.

- Women's development corporations have to gain access to open-ended financing.
- The financial institutions should provide more working capital assistance both for small scale venture and large scale ventures.
- Making provision of micro credit system and enterprise credit system to the women entrepreneurs at local level.
- Repeated gender sensitization programmes should be held to train financiers to treat women with dignity and respect as persons in their own right.
- Infrastructure, in the form of industrial plots and sheds, to set up industries is to be provided by state run agencies.
- Industrial estates could also provide marketing outlets for the display and sale of products made by women.
- A Women Entrepreneur's Guidance Cell set up to handle the various problems of women entrepreneurs all over the state.
- District Industries Centres and Single Window Agencies should make use of assisting women in their trade and business guidance.
- Programmes for encouraging entrepreneurship among women are to be extended at local level.
- Training in entrepreneurial attitudes should start at the high school level through well-designed courses, which build confidence through behavioral games.
- More governmental schemes to motivate women entrepreneurs to engage in small scale and large-scale business ventures.
- Involvement of Non Governmental Organizations in women entrepreneurial training programmes and counseling.

NEED OF THE HOUR

Women sector occupies nearly 45 per cent of the Indian population. The literary and educational status of women improved considerably during the past few decades. More and more higher educational and research institutions are imparting knowledge and specialisation. At this juncture, effective steps are needed to provide entrepreneurial awareness, orientation and skill development programmes to women. The institutions available at present are very limited. Moreover, their functions and opportunities available with them are not popularised much. It is urged that Government of India besides all state , should set up more vacational establishment to train women of all levels to train them in their core areas to ensure bright candidates to cross the border and lead many in our nation. They are that power needs to be pushed up with value added eduaction. The upcoming of hospitality industries , service and aviation are the areas they can come with colours.

The Global Philanthropy Forum aims to build a community of donors and social investors committed to international causes, and to inform, enable and enhance the strategic nature of their giving and social investing. By continually refreshing a lasting learning community, the Global Philanthropy Forum (GPF) seeks to increase the number of philanthropists who will be strategic in pursuit of international causes. We share a conviction that individuals are not only capable of advancing human security, environmental stewardship, and improved quality of life, but that they must.

WELCOME TO FIWE

Federation of Indian Women Entrepreneurs (FIWE), which is a National-level organization, founded in 1993, is today, one of India's Premier Institution for Women thoroughly devoted towards Entrepreneurship Development, having a large membership base of 15,000 individual members / professionals and more than 28 Member Associations spread throughout the country. The objective of the organization is to foster the Economic Empowerment of Women, particularly the SME segment, by helping them to become successful entrepreneurs and become a part of the mainstream industry. FIWE endeavours to provide: Networking platform for women, Technical know-how, Industry research and expertise, Skill development and training and brings the businesswomen on a Common Forum; and ensures that their opinions, ideas and visions are collectively and effectively taken up with policy makers and various other agencies respectively for the development of Enterprise in Women.

CONCLUSION

Independence brought promise of equality of opportunity in all sphere to the Indian women and laws guaranteeing for their equal rights of participation in political process and equal opportunities and rights in education and employment were enacted. But unfortunately, the government sponsored development activities have benefited only a small section of women. The large majority of them are still unaffected by change and development activities have benefited only a small section of women i.e. the urban middle class women. The large majority of them are still unaffected by change and development. The reasons are well sighted in the discussion part of this chapter. It is hoped that the suggestions forwarded in the chapter will help the entrepreneurs in particular and policy-planners in general to look into this problem and develop better schemes, developmental programmes and opportunities to the women folk to enter into more entrepreneurial ventures. This article here tries to recollect some of the successful women entrepreneurs like Ekta Kapoor, Creative Director, Balaji Telefilms, Kiran Mazumdar Shaw, CEO, Biocon, Shahnaz Husain and Vimalben M Pawale, Ex President, Sri Mahila Griha Udyog Lijjat Papad (SMGULP). Independence brought promise of equality of opportunity in all spheres to the Indian women and laws guaranteeing for their equal rights of participation in political process and equal opportunities and rights in education and employment were enacted. But unfortunately, the government sponsored developmental activities have benefitted only a small section of women i.e. the urban middle class women. The large majority of them are still unaffected by change and development. The present study of women entrepreneurs was undertaken at a crucial period when the question of women's contribution to development is being discussed at national level and attempts are being made to make women economically and socially independent. The study points out that entrepreneurship among women could not be developed as they caked confidence to start their own ventures. Social pressure and attitude of doubting women's capability and restricting their freedom of movement was found yet another hurdle. Financial organizations may also be held responsible for not encouraging women entrepreneurs.

REFERENCES

1. Jose P., Ajith Kumar. & Paul T.M., (1994) Entrepreneurship Development, Himalaya Publishing.
2. Medha Dubhashi Vinze (1987) Women Entrepreneurs In India: A Socio-economic Study of Delhi—1975-76, Mittal Publications, New Delhi.
3. Renuka V. (2001) Opportunities and Challenges for Women in Business, India Together, Online Report, Civil Society Information Exchange Pvt. Ltd.
4. Starcher, D. C. (1996). *Women Entrepreneurs: Catalysts for Transformation*. Retrieved July 6, 2001: http:// www.ebbf.org/ woman.htmls[10] (c20012695[11])
5. "The Female Poverty Trap." (2001, May 8). *The Economist*. Retrieved March 14, 2001: http://www.economist.com[12] (c20012022[13])
6. United Nations Industrial Development Organization (UNIDO). (1995a). "Women, Industry and Entrepreneurship." *Women in Industry Series*. Vienna, Austria: Author. Retrieved July 6, 20001: http://www.unido.org/doc/150401.htmls[15] (c20012668[16])
7. United Nations Industrial Development Organization (UNIDO). (1995b). "Women, Industry and Technology." *Women in Industry Series*. Vienna, Austria: Author. Retrieved July 6, 2001: http:// www.unido.org/doc/150401.htmls[15] (c20012666[18])
8. Women Entrepreneurs in Poorest Countries Face Formidable Challenges, Including Lack of Training, Credit, Say Speakers at Brussels Forum" [Press Release]. (2001, May 21). Retrieved July 6, 2001:http://www.unorg/News/Press/docs/2001/ dev2331.doc.html199. http://www.celcee.edu.

6

Knowledge Management and Women Entrepreneurship Development in India

Prof. Trilok Nath Shukla
Prof. Chumki Chatterjee

ABSTRACT

Knowledge management (KM) comprises a range of strategies and practices used in an organization to identify, create, represent, distribute, and enable adoption of insights and experiences. Such insights and experiences comprise knowledge, either embodied in individuals or embedded in organizational processes or practice. In terms of the enterprise, early collections of case studies recognized the importance of knowledge management dimensions of strategy, process, and measurement (Morey, Maybury & Thuraisingham 2002). In short, knowledge management programs can yield impressive benefits to individuals and organizations if they are purposeful, concrete, and action-oriented.

Women's entrepreneurship is both about women's position in society and the role of entrepreneurship in the same society. Women are faced with specific obstacles (such as family responsibilities) that have to be overcome in order to give them access to the same opportunities as men. In India women have become aware of their existence their rights and their work situation due to the knowledge gained through education. No doubt the progress is more visible among upper class families in urban cities. If we take the examples of Indian women entrepreneurs we will find that all have got a strong education background.

This chapter focuses on development of women entrepreneur's through knowledge.. The paper describes the status of women entrepreneurs and the problems faced by them when they ventured out to carve their own niche in the competitive world of business environment and how they succeeded in overcoming all the hurdles .

Key words: knowledge management, women entrepreneurs, knowledge economy, sex discrimination.

Introduction

Knowledge has the complexity of experience, which come about by seeing it from different perspectives. This is why training and education is difficult-one cannot count on one person's knowledge transferring to another. Knowledge is built from scratch by the learner through experience. Information is static, but knowledge is dynamic as it lives within us.

Knowledge management capabilities have a significant impact on innovation and organizational effectiveness. Now-a-days, competitive advantage no longer relies just on tangible assets and natural resources, but on how effectively firms manage knowledge. Intensifying global competition forces companies to innovate and improve or upgrade their competence frequently in order to maintain their competitive advantage in the global market. In general, this requires the fast exploring and acquiring of critical information and knowledge of the market and of its internal organization (Zalira & George, 2002). Wiklund and Shepherd (2003) suggest that future opportunities can be 'discovered' by combining an entrepreneurial orientation with knowledge management. When this combination can be effectively maintained by organizations, the likelihood of underpinning innovation and developing new competencies tends to be higher (Burstein, el al., 2003). By managing knowledge as a continuous process, organizations are able to meet existing and emerging needs, identify, exploit existing and acquired knowledge assets in order to develop new opportunities (Quintas et al., 1997; Carrillo et al., 2004 Furthermore, since knowledge is the key resource of competitive advantage, storing and protecting knowledge creates value for the organization (Berry, 2(X)0) so that they can keep innovating without fear of having imitated by their competitors. In addition, Ireland and Hitt (1999) proposed innovation and competence upgrading as two major factors for organizations to compete effectively in the market.

To survive and grow continuously, Gronhaug and Kaufmann (1988) suggest an organization should innovate in order to re-shape their competitive advantage. activities of an organization. In line with this, the present study places equal emphasis on products, process, and management in innovation. The improvement of coordination effects, the frequent commercialization of new products, a better ability to anticipate market change and so forth. Thus, having an entrepreneurial orientation should increase the capability of organizations to convert knowledge into innovation, upgrade their competence and make themselves generally more effective.

Moreover, market changes should be responded to by enforcing the application of existing knowledge all around the organization (Liao et al, 2003) that should, in turn, lead to an upgrading or improvement in its various organizational competences. In this respect, knowledge protection is critical effective competition in the market. Because the 'protection effect' of external laws, such as patents and copyright are not perfect (Berry, 2(XX)); an entrepreneurial-oriented organization is likely to be more enthusiastic about to taking protective measures to secure an advantage in innovation (Burton, 1999).

Indian Women Through Ages

Although the ancient system of education has produced many geniuses and still a major area of research, it was hardly egalitarian. Women and people of lower castes gradually lost their right to educate themselves. During the time of king

Ashoka women took part in religious preaching. According to Hiuen Tsang, the famous traveller of that time, Rajyashri, the sister of Harshavardhana was a distinguished scholar of her time. Another such example is the daughter of king Ashoka, Sanghmitra. She along with her brother Mahendra went to Sri Lanka to preach Buddhism. The status of women in Southern India was better than the North India. While in Northern India there were not many women administrators, in Southern India we can find some names that made women of that time proud. Priyaketaladevi, queen of Chalukya Vikramaditya ruled three villages. Another women named Jakkiabbe used to rule seventy villages. In South India women had representation in each and every field. Domingo Paes, famous Portuguese traveler testifies to it. He has written in his account that in Vijaynagar kingdom women were present in each and every field. He says that women could wrestle, blow trumpet and handle sword with equal perfection. Nuniz, another famous traveller to the South also agrees to it and says that women were employed in writing accounts of expenses, recording the affairs of kingdom, which shows that they were educated. There is no evidence of any public school in northern India but according to famous historian Ibn Batuta there were 13 schools for girls and 24 for boys in Honavar. There was one major evil present in South India of medieval time. It was the custom of Devadasis.

The spread of Jainism, Buddhism, Bhakti and Sufi movements did have some liberating effects on the condition of the women, sudras and atisudras. Medieval India was not women's age it is supposed to be the 'dark age' for them. Medieval India saw many foreign conquests, which resulted in the decline in women's status. When foreign conquerors like Muslims invaded India they brought with them their own culture. For them women was the sole property of her father, brother or husband and she does not have any will of her own. This type of thinking also crept into the minds of Indian people and they also began to treat their own women like this. One more reason for the decline in women's status and freedom was that original Indians wanted to shield their women-folk from the barbarous Muslim invaders. As polygamy was a norm for these invaders they picked up any women they wanted and kept her in their 'harems'. In order to protect them Indian women started using 'Purdah', (a veil), which covers body. Due to this reason their freedom also became affected. They were not allowed to move freely and this lead to the further deterioration of their status. These problems related with women resulted in changed mindset of people. Now they began to consider a girl as misery and a burden, which has to be shielded from the eyes of intruders and needs extra care. Whereas a boy child will not need such extra care and instead will be helpful as an earning hand. Thus a vicious circle started in which women was at the receiving end. All this gave rise to some new evils such as Child Marriage, Sati, Jauhar and restriction on girl education.

The girls of medieval India and especially Hindu society were not given formal education. They were given education related to household chores. But a famous Indian philosopher 'Vatsyayana' wrote that women were supposed to be perfect in sixty four arts which included cooking, spinning, grinding, knowledge of medicine, recitation and many more. Though these evils were present in medieval Indian society but they were mainly confined to Hindu society.But it is the English language and the reformation movements of the 19th century that had the most liberating effect in pre-independent India. Thus, the Britishers, although rightly criticized for devastating the Indian economy, can also be credited for bringing a revolution in the Indian education system.

The plight of women in medieval India and at the starting of modern India can be summed up in the words of great poet Rabindranath Tagore:"O Lord Why have you not given woman the right to conquer her destiny?Why does she have to wait head bowed,By the roadside, Waiting with tired patience, Hoping for a miracle in the morrow?"

Concept of Women Entrepreneur Enterprise

" A small scale industrial unit or industry—related service or business enterprise, managed by one or more women entrepreneurs in a concern, in which they will individually or jointly have a share capital of not less than 51 per cent as shareholders of the private limited company, members of co-operative society".

In this dynamic world, women entrepreneurs are an important part of the global quest for sustained economic development and social progress. In India, though women have played a key role in the society, their entrepreneurial ability has not been properly tapped due to the lower status of women in the society. It is only from the Fifth Five Year Plan (1974-78) onwards that their role has been explicitly recognized with a marked shift in the approach from women welfare to women development and empowerment. The development of women entrepreneurship has become an important aspect of our plan priorities. Several policies and programmes are being implemented for the development of women entrepreneurship in India.

There is a need for changing the mindset towards women so as to give equal rights as enshrined in the constitution. The progress towards gender equality is slow and is partly due to the failure to attach money to policy commitments. In the words of president APJ Abdul Kalam "empowering women is a prerequisite for creating a good nation, when women are empowered, society with stability is assured. Empowerment of women is essential as their thoughts and their value systems lead to the development of a good family, good society and ultimately a good nation."

When a woman is empowered it does not mean that another individual becomes powerless or is having less power. On the contrary, if a women is empowered her competencies towards decision- making will surely influence her family's behaviour.

In advanced countries, there is a phenomenon of increase in the number of self- employed women after the world war II. In USA, women own 25 per cent of all business, even though their sales on an average are less than two-fifths of those of other small business. In Canada, women own one-third of small business and in France it is one.

Women owned businesses are highly increasing in the economies of almost all countries. The hidden entrepreneurial potentials of women have gradually been changing with the growing sensitivity to the role and economic status in the society. Skill, knowledge and adaptability in business are the main reasons for women to emerge into business ventures.' Women Entrepreneur' is a person who accepts challenging role to meet her personal needs and become economically independent. A strong desire to do something positive is an inbuilt quality of entrepreneurial women, who is capable of contributing values in both family and social life. With the advent of media, women are aware of their own traits, rights and also the work situations. The glass ceilings are shattered and women are found indulged in every line of business from pepped to power cables. The challenges and opportunities provided to the women of digital era are growing rapidly that the job seekers are turning into job creators. They are flourishing as designers, interior decorators, exporters, publishers, garment manufacturers and still exploring new avenues of economic participation. In India, although women constitute the majority of the total population, the entrepreneurial world is still a male dominated one. Women in advanced nations are recognized and are more prominent in the business world. But the Indian women entrepreneurs are facing some major constraints like Lack of confidence, socio-cultural barriers, Market-oriented risks, Knowledge in Business Administration and Awareness about the financial assistance.

The additional business opportunities that are recently approaching for women enterpreuners are Eco-friendly technology, Bio-technology, IT enabled enterprises, Event Management, Tourism industry, Telecommunication, Plastic materials, Vermiculture, Sericulture, Floriculture, Herbal and healthcare and food, fruits and vegetable processing.

Empowering women entrepreneurs is essential for achieving the goals of sustainable development and the bottlenecks hindering their growth must be eradicated to entitle full participation in the business. Apart from training programmes, newsletters, mentoring, trade fairs and exhibitions also can be a source for entrepreneurial development. As a result, the desired outcomes of the business are quickly achieved and more of remunerative business opportunities are found. Hence forth, promoting entrepreneurship among women is certainly a short-cut to rapid economic growth and development.

Development of Women Entrepreneurs in India

Soon after gaining independence in 1947, making education available to all had become a priority for the government. As discrimination on the basis of caste and gender has been a major impediment in the healthy development of the Indian society, they have been made unlawful by the Indian constitution. The 86th constitutional amendment has also made elementary education a fundamental right for the children between the age group—6 to 14.

In order to develop the higher education system, the government had established the University Grants Commission in 1953. The primary role of UGC has been to regulate the standard and spread of higher education in India. The higher education system in India comprises of more than 17000 colleges, 20 central universities, 217 State Universities, 106 Deemed to Universities and 13 institutes of National importance. This number will soon inflate as the setting up of 30 more central universities, 8 new IITs, 7 IIMs and 5 new Indian Institutes of Science are now proposed.

As education is the means for bringing socio- economic transformation in a society, . Efforts are also being taken to improve the access to higher education among the women of India by setting up various educational institutes exclusively for them or reserving seats in the already existing institutes.

The status of women in modern India is a sort of a paradox. If on one hand she is at the peak of ladder of success, on the other hand she is mutely suffering the violence afflicted on her by her own family members. As compared with past women in modern times have achieved a lot but in reality they have to still travel a long way. Their path is full of roadblocks. The women have left the secured domain of their home and are now in the battlefield of life, fully armored with their talent. They had proven themselves. But in India they are yet to get their dues. The sex ratio of India shows that the Indian society is still prejudiced against female. There are 933 females per thousand males in India according to the census of 2001, which is much below the world average of 990 females.

According to last census held in 2001, the percentage of female literacy in the country is 54.16 per cent.The literacy rate in the country has increased from 18.33 per cent in 1951 to 65.38 per cent as per 2001 census. The female literacy rate has also increased from 8.86 per cent in 1951 to 54.16 per cent. It is noticed that the female literacy rate during the period 1991-2001 increased by 14.87 per cent whereas male literacy rate rose by 11.72 per cent. Hence the female literacy rate actually increased by 3.15 per cent more compared to male literacy rate.

At present, women involvement in economic activities is marked by a low work participation rate, excessive concentration in the unorganized sector and employment in less skilled jobs. Any strategy aimed at economic development will be lop-sided without involving women who constitute half of the world population. Evidence has unequivocally established that entrepreneurial spirit is not a male prerogative. Women entrepreneurship has gained momentum in the last three decades with the increase in the number of women enterprises and their substantive contribution to economic growth. The industrial performance of Asia-Pacific region propelled by Foreign Direct Investment, technological innovations and manufactured exports has brought a wide range of economic and social opportunities to women entrepreneurs.

If we classify the women entrepreneurs in India they can be divided into three categories.

First Category will include the organizations established in big cities which require the women having higher level technical and professional qualifications with sound financial positions and deals with nontraditional Items. The *Second* Category defines those industries which are established in cities and towns and deals with both traditional and nontraditional items but require sufficient education. The examples are kindergarten, crèches, beauty parlours, health clinic etc. The *Third* Category include Illiterate women who are financially week and are Involved in family business such as Agriculture, Horticulture, Animal Husbandry, Dairy, Fisheries, Agro Forestry, Handloom, Power loom etc.

Problems of Women Entrepreneurs in India

Women in India are faced many problems to get ahead their life in business A kind of patriarchal male dominant social order is the building block to them in their way towards business success. The financial institutions are skeptical about the entrepreneurial abilities of women. The bankers consider women loonies as higher risk than men loonies. The bankers put unrealistic and unreasonable securities to get loan to women entrepreneurs. According to a report by the United Nations Industrial Development Organization (UNIDO), "despite evidence that women's loan repayment rates are higher than men's, women still face more difficulties in obtaining credit," often due to discriminatory attitudes of banks and informal lending groups (UNIDO, 1995b).

Women's family obligations also bar them from becoming successful entrepreneurs in both developed and developing nations. "Having primary responsibility for children, home and older dependent family members, few women can devote all their time and energies to their business" (Starcher, 1996). Indian women give more emphasis to family ties and relationships. Married women have to make a fine balance between business and home. More over the business success is depends on the support the family members extended to women in the business process and management. Another argument is that women entrepreneurs have low-level management skills. They have to depend on office staffs and intermediaries, to get things done, especially, the marketing and sales side of business. Marketing means mobility and confidence in dealing with the external world, both of which women have been discouraged from developing by social conditioning. Despite the fact that women entrepreneurs are good in keeping their service prompt and delivery in time, due to lack of organizational skills compared to male entrepreneurs women have to face constraints from competition. The confidence to travel across day and night and even different regions and states are less found in women compared to male entrepreneurs. This shows the low level freedom of expression and freedom of mobility of the women entrepreneurs.

There exists a strong connection between the presence of role models and the emergence of entrepreneurs (Shapero & Sokol, 1982) and women as they historically have not been present as entrepreneurs in general lack close role models. Role models are persons that by their attitudes, behaviours and actions establish the desirability and credibility of a choice (in this case becoming an entrepreneur) for an individual. Furthermore, the influence of role models is one's aspirations and choices tend to be more influenced by persons of the same sex (Deaux & Lafrance, 1998).

All stages in entrepreneurship are dependent on relevant experience, from the identification of opportunities to the execution of running a business. Human capital refers here to the knowledge and skills that assist people in successfully discovering and exploiting opportunities (cf. Davidsson & Honig, Forthcoming; Snell and Dean, 1992). recent research on developed economies has identified a potential problem when it comes to women's entrepreneurship: highly educated women seem to choose other career options than self-employment and entrepreneurship. Entrepreneurship is therefore relatively more dominated by unskilled women or very skilled and already wealthy women. Moreover Women have in general a lower social position than men, which affects the kind of networks they can access or are part of. For business it is as important to have weak-tie networks as strong-ties (Aldrich & Zimmer, 1986b; Burt, 2000; Granovetter, 1985; Granovetter, 1973). The strong and personal networks that women traditionally engage in are well suited to purposes linked to the family related tasks that may prove to be a hindrance in the marketplace (Lin, 1999). Thus, women differ to men in the kind of networks they use and in the social capital available to them through the network. Women have therefore less access to critical resources, support and information needed to successfully start and manage a new firm compared to men.

A prerequisite for starting a firm is to have capital in terms of financial assets and in terms of relevant knowledge assets. Women's position in society has led to a lack of assets in both these aspects.

Knowledge of alternative source of raw materials availability and high negotiation skills are the basic requirement to run a business. Getting the raw materials from different source with discount prices is the factor that determines the profit margin. Lack of knowledge of availability of the raw materials and low-level negotiation and bargaining skills are the factors, which affect women entrepreneur's business adventures.. Knowledge of latest technological changes, know how, and education level of the person are significant factor that affect business. The literacy rate of women in India is found at low level compared to male population. Many women in developing nations lack the education needed to spur successful entrepreneurship. They are ignorant of new technologies or unskilled in their use, and often unable to do research and gain the necessary training (UNIDO, 1995b, p.1). Although great advances are being made in technology, many women's illiteracy, structural difficulties, and lack of access to technical training prevent the technology from being beneficial or even available to females ("Women Entrepreneurs in Poorest Countries," 2001). According to The Economist, this lack of knowledge and the continuing treatment of women as second-class citizens keep them in a pervasive cycle of poverty ("The Female Poverty Trap," 2001). The studies indicates that uneducated women don't have the knowledge of measurement and basic accounting.

Low-level risk taking attitude is another factor affecting women folk decision to get into business. Low-level education provides low-level self-confidence and self-reliance to the women folk to engage in business, which is continuous risk taking and strategic cession making profession. Investing money, maintaining the operations and ploughing back money for surplus generation requires high risk taking attitude, courage and confidence. Though the risk tolerance ability of the women folk in day-to-day life is high compared to male members, while in business it is found opposite to that.

Another recurring obstacle for women to engage in entrepreneurship is the perceived lack of time or competing demands on time. Because women are responsible for so many different domestic chores and the raising of children, they do not have enough free time to develop either their entrepreneurial skills to become entrepreneurs or to develop an existing business. The lack of free time does not allow them time to travel to support institutions, banks and other finance houses for advice and information on credit, to attend training programmes to acquire skills, or to seek out better customers or suppliers.

A specific problem of women entrepreneurs seems to be their inability to achieve growth especially sales growth (Du Rietz & Henrekson, 2000).Finally high production cost of some business operations adversely affects the development of women entrepreneurs. The installation of new machineries during expansion of the productive capacity and like similar factors dissuades the women entrepreneurs from venturing into new areas.

Initiatives for Women Entrepreneurs in India

The 11th plan is all about education, where the government will be spending 67 billion dollars on education. About 6,000 crore have been approved by the cabinet to build a knowledge network. This network is about connecting 1,500 locations. The programme is about connectivity of the nodes. The schools, all universities and R&D institutes will be connected and scientists will begin to collaborate, and teachers will be able to share the resources. This programme has already been implemented, 15 nodes have been connected and are working. Within 18 months, all the nodes will be connected and made operational. This will be the mother of all networks.

The Supportive Measures for Women's Economic Activities and Entrepreneurship is provided by direct & indirect financial support, Yojna schemes and programmes, Technological training and awards and Federations and associations. The direct and Indirect Financial Support is provided by Nationalized banks, State finance corporation, State industrial development corporation, District industries centers, Differential rate schemes, Mahila Udyug Needhi scheme , Small Industries Development Bank of India (SIDBI) and State Small Industrial Development Corporations (SSIDCs) .Yojna Schemes and Programme includes Nehru Rojgar Yojna, Jacamar Rojgar Yojna,

TRYSEM and DWACRA .Technological Training and Awards includes Stree Shakti Package by SBI, Entrepreneurship Development Institute of India, Trade Related Entrepreneurship Assistance and Development (TREAD), National Institute of Small Business Extension Training (NSIBET) and Women's University of Mumbai. Federations and Associations includes National Alliance of Young Entrepreneurs (NAYE), India Council of Women Entrepreneurs, New Delhi, Self Employed Women's Association (SEWA), Association of Women Entrepreneurs of Karnataka (AWEK), World Association of Women Entrepreneurs (WAWE) and Associated Country Women of the World (ACWW).

Role of Knowledge Management

Jack Welch, the legendary former CEO of GE, wrote in 1989, "The competitive world of the nineties will make the eighties look like a walk in the park. To win we have to find the key to dramatic, sustained productivity growth... We have to turn in the nineties to the software of our companies, to the culture that drives them... We have to move from the incremental to radical, toward a fundamental revolution in our approach to productivity and to work itself — a revolution that must touch every single person in the organization every business day."

Knowledge Management (KM) comprises a range of strategies and practices used in an organization to identify, create, represent, distribute, and enable adoption of insights and experiences. Such insights and experiences comprise knowledge, either embodied in individuals or embedded in organizational processes or practice. Knowledge management has also become a cornerstone in emerging business strategies such as Service Lifecycle Management (SLM) with companies increasingly turning to software vendors to enhance their efficiency in industries including, but not limited to, the aviation industry.

Modern software and networking enables producers and consumers unprecedented ease in creating and sharing digitized knowledge. The knowledge economy will Abstract away from products and services and focus on consumer experience itself, using products/services as props. Marketing will rise in importance in the knowledge economy because it is closest to the study of customer experience. However, the "efficiency" competencies function as key inputs into customer experience. Companies need to empower employees with customer information and decision making authority, so employees can enable differentiating customer experiences.

The knowledge economy transforms roles between all parties in the economy by extensive collaboration where buyers will tap into sellers' resources to participate in the design and delivery of products and services and likewise, sellers will access buyers' knowledge about experiences and emerging desires. This will benefit buyers and sellers immensely and bring significant wealth. The knowledge economy will bring a quantum leap in productivity over the industrial economy as all players gain competence in creating, managing and sharing digitized knowledge.Consumers are becoming increasingly sophisticated at managing information and creating and sharing digitized knowledge. They are developing the skills to interact with producers as equal partners.

In the industrial economy, human work was encapsulated in products and productized services, which included insight into consumers' lives. In the knowledge economy, digitized knowledge will add to producers' insights into consumers' lives; hence the ability to focus on experience, which is iterative.

Corporate Divas of India

Kiran Majumdar Shaw the richest Indian woman is the MD of Biocon India. She is the wealthiest entrepreneur of India . She is the first female master brewer and the richest woman in India. Shaw obtained her Honors degree in Zoology from Bangalore University. Then she went to Ballarat University to study brewery. She started her firm Biocon India in 1978 in her garage. When she applied for loan to the banks, she was turned down. At that time, biotechnology was not known in India and she was a female and her company did not have much assets. With her hard work and determination she overcome all these obstacles and turned Biocon into the biggest biopharmaceutical firm in India.

Indra Nooyi is Madras born woman was a straight "A" student in her school. Nooyi did her bachelors from Madras Christian College and MBA from Indian Institute of Management, Calcutta. Nooyi then went to USA and attended Yale University. From Yale, she obtained degree on management. This brilliant corporate woman started her career in Boston Consulting Group and moved on to Motorola and Asea Brown Boveri. She joined Pepsi Co. in 1994. She turned the company into a bold risk taker. In 1998, Pepsi acquired Tropicana. In 1997, Pepsi started its own fast food chain. In 2001, she became President of Pepsi Cola. Wall Street Journal included her name in their top 50 women to watch in 2005. Fortune magazine declared her 11th most powerful women in business.

Lalita Gupte and Kalpana Morparia are Joint Managing Directors of ICICI Bank, the second largest bank of India. Lalita Gupte created a formidable global presence of what was once a native development finance institution. Account-holders can now bank at ICICI branches in UK, the Far East, West Asia and Canada. With ICICI since 1971, Gupte was the first woman to be inducted on the board in 1984 .Lalita Gupte holds a Master's Degree in Management Studies from Jamnalal Bajaj Institute of Management Studies. She joined ICICI Bank in 1971. Her reason behind success is her supportive family. She got great support from her husband and in laws.

Ms. Kalpana Morparia is a graduate in law from Mumbai University. She joined ICICI in 1975 as a senior legal officer. In 1996, she became General Manager. She became Executive Director in 2001. In 1999, for her contribution in Finance and Banking sector in India, Indian Merchants' Chamber awarded her.

Vidya Manohar Chhabria the wife of late Manohar Rajaram Chhabria, is now leading Jumbo Group, a Dubai based $1.5 billion business conglomerate. She became chairperson of the company after the death of her husband in 2002. She runs the business with the help of her three daughters. She was ranked 38th most powerful women by the Fortune magazine in 2003.

Anu Aga became the Chairperson of Thermax Engineering after the death of her husband Rohinton Aga. The company's condition was critical at that time. Its share price dipped to ₹ 36 from ₹400. Anu Aga, the then Director of Human Resource, Thermax, was compelled to take charge of the company. In order to make the company profitable, she brought a consultant from abroad and restructured the company. The strategy worked and the company saw profit again. She stepped down from the post of chairperson in 2004. Now, she spends most of her time in social activities. Bombay Management Association awarded her Management Woman Achiever of the Year Award 2002-2003.

Simone Tata With her visions, she changed a small unknown cosmetics company, one of the subsidiaries of Tata Oil Mills, into one of the leading cosmetic companies of India. Lakme changed the face of Indian fashion and cosmetics forever. For her success, Simone N. Tata is also known as Cosmetic Czarina of India. Simone joined Lakme in 1961 and became Chairperson in 1982. The company is now sold to Hindustan Liver. Simone is now heading Trent Limited another subsidiary of the Tata Company.

Indu Jain has many identities: spiritualist, entrepreneur, humanist, educationalist, great lover of art and culture. She was the Chairman of the The Times Group, the biggest and the most powerful media house in India. The company was bought from a British group. Now, her two sons Samir and Vineet are running the company. Among the major products of the company, The Times of India, the largest selling English daily newspaper of the world. In 2000, Jain delivered speech at the Millenium World Peace Summit of Religious and Spiritual Leaders.

Priya Paul finished her Bachelor's in Economics from USA. She got into her family business at the age of 24 after her father Surrendra Paul was assassinated in 1990. Appeejay Surrendra Group has several subsidiaries such as, tea, hotel, shipping, retail, real estate and financial services. At present, Priya is the Chairperson of Appeejay Park Hotels.

Sulajja Firodia Motwani is the Joint Managing Director of Kinetic, and the Managing Director of Kinetic Finance. Her grandfather founded this company. He was a very well known figure in the Indian auto industry. Sulajja did her MBA in America. Later, she worked in Barra International, a California based investment consultancy firm, for four years and then returned to India and joined her family business.

She travels a lot around India and likes to deal face to face with people. This is how she tries to understand the market in her country.

Neelam Dhawan has become a pioneering figure in the IT industry of India. Neelam Dhawan has been working in the Indian IT field for the last twenty two years. She is the new Managing Director of Microsoft India. Before coming to Microsoft, she worked in all the top IT companies in India such as HP, IBM and HCL.

Fortune magazine listed ***Naina Lal Kidwai,*** Investment Banker as one of the world's most powerful businesswomen in 2003. India Inc recognises her as one of its most powerful investment bankers. But Naina Lal Kidwai, HSBC's deputy CEO, can't be reduced to simple woman-banker equations; her professional vision transcends gender.

Shahnaz Husain, Herbal Beauty Queen **is** the *"Estee Lauder* of India", with even famous department stores like Galleries Lafayette in Paris, Harrods and Selfridges in London and Bloomingdales in New York stocking her cosmetics, creams and lotions.

Ekta Kapoor can be aptly called as the reigning queen of Indian television industry. The serials produced by her company Balaji Telefilms are a great hit with the masses and are dominating all the major T.V. channels in India. She was Awarded with Ernst & Young (E&Y) Startup Entrepreneuro of the year award in 2001.

CONCLUSION

By general human capital we mean access to basic education (in developing economies) as well as the sex discrimination in science and technology (in developed economies). In both cases, women tend to lack the skills and experience that lead them to a higher probability of identifying entrepreneurial opportunities whit a high potential of survival and growth. In developing economies we now know that the natural science and engineering sector has become increasingly important for economic growth. Unfortunately, women are largely excluded from this sector.

Entrepreneurship among women, no doubt improves the wealth of the nation in general and of the family in particular. Women entrepreneurs play an important role in the entrepreneurial economy, both in their ability to create jobs for themselves and to create jobs for others. Women today are more willing to take up activities that were once considered the preserve of men, and have proved that they are second to no one with respect to contribution to the growth of the economy. Women entrepreneurship must be moulded properly with entrepreneurial traits and skills to meet the changes in trends, challenges global markets and also be competent enough to sustain and strive for excellence in the entrepreneurial arena.

Policy makers must foster the networking of associations and encourage co-operation and partnerships among national and international networks and facilitate entrepreneurial endeavours by women in the economy.

Women's entrepreneurship is both about women's position in society *and* the role of entrepreneurship in the same society. Women are faced with specific obstacles (such as family responsibilities) that have to be overcome in order to give them access to the same opportunities as men. Also, in some countries, women may experience obstacles with respect to holding property and entering contracts. Increased participation of women in the labour force is a prerequisite for improving the position of women in society and self-employed women. Indian women have mastered anything and everything which a woman can dream of. But she still has to go a long way to achieve equal status in the minds of Indian men.

REFERENCES

1. Acs, Z. J., Audretsch, D. B., & Feldman, M. P. 1994. R & D Spillovers and Recipient Firm Size. *The Review of Economics and Statistics*, Vol. 76 No. (2), pp. 336-340.
2. Adler, P. S., & Kwon, S.-W. 2002. Social Capital: Prospects for a New Concept. *Academy of Management Review*, Vol. 27 No.(1), pp.17-40.

3. Addicott, Rachael; McGivern, Gerry; Ferlie, Ewan (2006). "Networks, Organizational Learning and Knowledge Management: NHS Cancer Networks". *Public Money & Management* Vol.26No. (2), pp.87–94.

4. Andrus, D. Calvin (2005). "The Wiki and the Blog: Toward a Complex Adaptive Intelligence Community". *Studies in Intelligence* 49 (3).

5. Achterbergh, Jan & Vriens, Dirk (May-June 2002). "Managing Viable Knowledge." *Systems Research and Behavioral Science.* V19 i3 p 223(19).

6. Baumol, W. J. 1993. *Entrepreneurship, Management, and the Structure of Payoffs.* Cambridge, Massachusetts: The MIT Press.

7. Becker, G. S. 1964. *Human Capital.* Chicago: University of Chicago Press.

8. Booker, Lorne; Bontis, Nick; Serenko, Alexander (2008). "The Relevance of Knowledge Management and Intellectual Capital Research". *Knowledge and Process Management* Vol.15 No. (4), pp.235–246.

9. Brush, C. G. 1992. Research on Women Business Owners: Past trends, a New Perspective and Future Directions. *Entrepreneurship Theory and Practice,* Vol.16 No.(4), pp.5-30.

10. Delmar, F, & Shane, S. Forthcoming. Does Planning Facilitate Product Development in New Ventures? *Strategic Management Journal.*

11. Dhameja S K (2002) , Women Entrepreneurs : Opportunities, performance, problems, Deep publications (p) Ltd, New Delhi.

12. Larson, A., & Starr, J. A. 1993. A Network Model of Organizational Formation. *Entrepreneurship Theory & Practice,* 17(2): 5-15.

13. Lent, R. W., brown, S. D., & Hackett, G. 1994. Toward a Unified Social Cognitive Theory.

14. Of Career and Academic Interests, Choice, and Performance. *Journal of Vocational Behavior,* 45: 79-122.

15. Myers, S. C., & Majluf, N. S. 1984. Corporate Financing and Investment Decisions When Firms Have Information That Investors Do Not Have. *Journal of Financial Economics,* 187-221.

16. Rajendran N (2003) , "Problems and Prospects of Women Entrepreneurs" SEDME, Vol. 30 No. 4 December.

17. Rao Padala Shanmukha (2007) "Enterpreneurship Development Among Women: A Case Study of Self Help Groups in Srikakulam District, Andhra Pradesh" The Icfai Journal of Enterpreneurship Development Vol. 1,V, No.1.

18. Sharma Sheetal (2006) " Educated Women , Powered, Women" *Yojana* Vol.50, No.12.

19 Shiralashetti A S and Hugar S S " Problem and Prospects of Women Entrepreneurs In North Karnataka District: A case study" The Icfai Journal of Entrepreneurship Development Vol.1v No. 2.

20. Todaro, M. P. 2000. *Economic Development* (7th ed.). Reading, Mass.: Addison Wesly Longman Inc.

21. Uzzi, B. 1997. Social Structure and Competition in Interfirm Networks: The Paradox of Embeddedness. *Administrative Science Quarterly*, 42: 35-67.

7

Rural Women Entrepreneurship in India
Opportunities and Challenges

Dr. S. K. Chaudhury
Dr. K. R. Swain
Dr. N. Nayak

ABSTRACT

In India majority of people live in rural areas and they are engaged in different agricultural and allied activities to maintain their livelihood. Around half of the rural population represents women communities. In the men dominated society rural women have acquired a very low status in their social life. In the economic activities and decision making process in their position is negligible. For productivity, employment generation and income orientation their activities are hindered by many socio-economic constraints. Majority of women do not undertake entrepreneurial ventures. There is need to strengthen and stremline the sectors by harnessing their power towards nation building and to attain accelerated economic growth. Women are engaged in a wide variety of occupations especially in the unorganized sector. in rural in the hand-looms, and producing handicrafts mostly as low paid wage earners or unpaid family workers.

This chapter explains the rural entrepreneurship, its opportunities and its challenges for rural entrepreneurship. It also highlights the rural women entrepreneurship, its opportunities, its challenges and opportunities requied for rural women entrepreneurship and also various contraints of women entrepreneurship. Furthermore it highlights entrepreneurship development among rural women through micro credit and women entrepreneurship in India.

PROLOGUE

The entrepreneurs may be from anywhere, but their enterprises have to be located in a rural area, using mainly local resources both material as well as human. Also, the enterprises have to be located in a rural area though it need not be actually using 100% local material and human resources. But the large portion of material used should be locally procured and an appreciable number of people should be engaged in the production and from rural areas .

Entrepreneurship has gained greater significance at global level under changing economic scenario. Global economy in general and Indian economy in particular is poised for accelerated growth driven by entrepreneurship. In the environment of super mall culture we find plenty of scope for entrepreneurship in trading and manufacturing.

DENOTATION OF ENTREPRENEUR

An entrepreneur is a person who is able to look at the environment, identify opportunities to improve the environmental resources and implement action to maximize those opportunities (Robert E. Nelson) it is important to bear in mind the entrepreneurial skills that will be needed to improve the quality of life for individuals, families and communities and to sustain a healthy economy and environment. Taking this into consideration, we will find that each of the traditional definitions has its own weakness (Tyson, Petrin, Rogers, 1994, p. 4).

The first definition leaves little room for innovations that are not on the technological or organizational cutting edge, such as, adaptation of older technologies to a developing-country context, or entering into export markets already tapped by other firms. Defining entrepreneurship as risk-taking neglects other major elements of what we usually think of as entrepreneurship, such as a well-developed ability to recognize unexploited market opportunities.

Entrepreneurship as a stabilizing force limits entrepreneurship to reading markets disequilibria, while entrepreneurship defined as owning and operating a business, denies the possibility of entrepreneurial behaviour by non-owners, employees and managers who have no equity stake in the business. Therefore, the most appropriate definition of entrepreneurship that would fit into the rural development context, argued here, is the broader one, the one which defines entrepreneurship as: "a force that mobilizes other resources to meet unmet market demand", "the ability to create and build something from practically nothing", "the process of creating value by pulling together a unique package of resources to exploit an opportunity".

It combines definitions of entrepreneurship by Jones and Sakong, 1980; Timmons, 1989; Stevenson, et al., 1985. Entrepreneurship so defined, pertains to any new organization of productive factors and not exclusively to innovations that are on the technological or organizational cutting edge, it pertains to entrepreneurial activities both within and outside the organization. Entrepreneurship need not involve anything new from a global or even national perspective, but rather the adoption of new forms of business organizations, new technologies and new enterprises producing goods not previously available at a location (Petrin, 1991).

This is why entrepreneurship is considered to be a prime mover in development and why nations, regions and communities that actively promote entrepreneurship development, demonstrate much higher growth rates and consequently higher levels of development than nations, regions and communities whose institutions, politics and culture hinder entrepreneurship. An entrepreneurial economy, whether on the national, regional or community level, differs significantly from a non-entrepreneurial economy in many respects, not only by its economic structure and its economic vigorousness, but also by the social vitality and quality of life which it offers with a consequent attractiveness to people.

Economic structure is very dynamic and extremely competitive due to the rapid creation of new firms and the exit of 'old' stagnant and declining firms Redefining entrepreneurship and innovation Succeeding as an entrepreneur and an innovator in today's world is vastly different from what it was earlier. Organizations will face seven trends in the next decade as they flight to survive, grow and remain competitive.

- Speed and uncertainty will prevail.
- Technology will continue to disrupt and enable.
- Demographics will dictate much of what happens in business.
- Loyalty will erode.
- Work will be done anywhere, anytime.
- Employment as we know it will disappear.

RURAL ENTREPRENEURSHIP

Rural entrepreneur succeeding as an entrepreneur and an innovator in today's world is vastly different from what it was earlier. Besides the existing generation of entrepreneurship also is passing through the transition period. They experience financial resource limitation to promote or to develop a venture and there is also look of research and innovation to meat with marketing challenges. Indian rural economy is also experiencing behavior of entrepreneurial. Aim of most farmers is to earn profits from farming as from any other business, if he determines the objectives. A farm business necessary requires deliberate decision and proper investment, after assessing risk and available resources to maximize profit. There for entrepreneurship is not simply adoption of new activity but it is transformation of a person from traditional of modern India is known as "Home spices" and is in fact the largest producer, consumer and exporter of spices in the world. Though, cumin cultivation requires more inputs and production prices are high but last two years monetary output is uncertain. It is also sensitive crop to many disease, pest and also highly risky crop considering natural hazards, as well as the day to day fluctuating wholesale price index. Organizations will face seven trends in the next decade as they flight to survive, grow and remain competitive.

- Speed and uncertainty will prevail.
- Technology will continue to disrupt and enable.
- Demographics will dictate much of what happens in business.
- Work will be done anywhere, anytime.
- Employment as we know it will disappear.

OPPORTUNITIES FOR RURAL ENTREPRENEURS

- Crashed Scheme for Rural Development
- Food for Work Programme
- National Rural Employment Programme
- Regional Rural Development Centres
- Entrepreneurship Development institute of India
- Bank of Technology
- Rural Innovation Funding
- Social Rural Entrepreneurship.

CHALLENGES FOR RURAL ENTREPRENEURS

- Growth of Mall Culture
- Poor Assistance
- Power Failure
- Lack of Technical know-how
- Capacity Utilization
- Infrastructure Sickness

WOMEN ENTREPRENEUR

Women entrepreneurs have been making a significant impact in all segments of the economy in India, Canada, Great Britain, Germany, Australia and the United States. The areas chosen by women are retail trade, restaurants, hotels, education, cultural, cleaning, insurance and manufacturing The New Thrust suggests following two factors pulling or pushing women in an entrepreneurship Factors leading women to be an entrepreneur: Women entrepreneurs choose a Women takes up business enterprises to Profession as a challenge and an get over financial difficulties and respond- adventure with an urge to do some - sibility is thrust on them due to family - thing new, liking for business and circumstances. to have an independent occupation. With the spread of education and new approaches/awareness, women entrepreneurs are achieving higher level of 3E's, namely: (i) Engineering (ii) Electronics (iii) Energy. Though we should not forget certain Psycho-Social Barriers which hinders the growth of women entrepreneurs.

OPPORTUNITIES

- Free entry into world trade
- Improved risk taking ability
- Governments of nations withdrawn some restrictions
- Technology and inventions spread into the world
- Encouragement to innovations and inventions
- Promotion of healthy completions among nations
- Consideration increase in government assistance for international trade
- Establishment of other national and international institutes to support business among nations of the world
- Benefits of specialization
- Social and cultural development

CHALLENGES

- Problems of raising equity capital
- Difficulty in borrowing fund.
- Thought-cut completions endangered existence of small companies.
- Problems of availing raw-materials.
- Problems of obsolescence of indigenous technology

- Increased pollutions ecological imbalanced
- Problems of TRIPS and TRIMS
- Exploitation of small and poor countries, etc.

SUGGESTIONS

- Govt. should provide separate financial fund of women's entrepreneur
- We should provide her special infrastructure facilities whatever she deeds
- Govt. should arrange special training programmes of women entrepreneurship
- Govt. should felicitate top ranked women's entrepreneur
- Women entrepreneur should more competitive and efficient in the local & international market
- Use should invite successful women entrepreneurs from foreign countries

CONSTRAINTS WOMEN ENTREPRENEUR

Women owned businesses are highly increasing in the economies of almost all countries. The hidden entrepreneurial potentials of women have gradually been changing with the growing sensitivity to the role and economic status in the society. Skill, knowledge and adaptability in business are the main reasons for women to emerge into business ventures.' Women Entrepreneur' is a person who accepts challenging role to meet her personal needs and become economically independent. A strong desire to do something positive is an inbuilt quality of entrepreneurial women, who is capable of contributing values in both family and social life. With the advent of media, women are aware of their own traits, rights and also the work situations. The glass ceilings are shattered and women are found indulged in every line of business from pepped to power cables. The challenges and opportunities provided to the women of digital era are growing rapidly that the job seekers are turning into job creators. They are flourishing as designers, interior decorators, exporters, publishers, garment manufacturers and still exploring new avenues of economic participation. In India, although women constitute the majority of the total population, the entrepreneurial world is still a male dominated one. Women in advanced nations are recognized and are more prominent in the business world. But the Indian women entrepreneurs are facing some major constraints like:

a) *Lack of confidence:* In general, women lack confidence in their strength and competence. The family members and the society are reluctant to stand beside their entrepreneurial growth. To a certain extent, this situation is changing among Indian women and yet to face a tremendous change to increase the rate of growth in entrepreneurship;

b) *Socio-cultural barriers:* Women's family and personal obligations are sometimes a great barrier for succeeding in business career. Only few women are able to manage both home and business efficiently, devoting enough time to perform all their responsibilities in priority;

c) *Market-oriented risks:* Stiff competition in the market and lack of mobility of women make the dependence of women entrepreneurs on middleman indispensable. Many business women find it difficult to capture the market and make their products popular. They are not fully aware of the changing market conditions and hence can effectively utilize the services of media and internet.

d) *Motivational factors:* Self motivation can be realized through a mind set for a successful business, attitude to take up risk and behaviour towards the business society by shouldering the social responsibilities. Other factors are family support, Government policies, financial assistance from public and private institutions and also the environment suitable for women to establish business units;

e) *Knowledge in Business Administration:* Women must be educated and trained constantly to acquire the skills and knowledge in all the functional areas of business management. This can facilitate women to excel in decision making process and develop a good business network;

f) *Awareness about the financial assistance:* Various institutions in the financial sector extend their maximum support in the form of incentives, loans, schemes etc. Even then every woman entrepreneur may not be aware of all the assistance provided by the institutions. So the sincere efforts taken towards women entrepreneurs may not reach the entrepreneurs in rural and backward areas;

g) *Exposed to the training programs:* Training programs and workshops for every type of entrepreneur is available through the social and welfare associations, based on duration, skill and the purpose of the training programmes. Such programs are really useful to new, rural and young entrepreneurs who want to set up a small and medium scale unit on their own;

h) *Identifying the available resources:* Women are hesitant to find out the access to cater their needs in the financial and marketing areas. In spite of the mushrooming growth of associations, institutions, and the schemes from the government side, women are not enterprising and dynamic to optimize the resources in the form of reserves, assets mankind or business volunteers;

ENTREPRENEURSHIP DEVELOPMENT AMONG RURAL WOMEN THROUGH MICRO CREDIT

SHGs are of recent origin in rural India to helping more than 17 million women from villages improve their incomes , educate their children , and buy assets . SHGs have also helped women campaign against oppressive social practices and become a force of development in their villages Before 1990's credit schemes for rural women were almost negligible . The concept of women's credit was born on the insistence by women oriented studies that highlighted the discrimination and struggle of women in having access to credit.

Micro credits are enough for innovative and hard working micro entrepreneurs to start small business such as making handicraft items. From the income of these small business the borrowers of micro credit can enjoy better life, food, shelter, healthcare and education for their families and above all these small earnings will provide a hope for better future. There are certain misconceptions about the poor rural women that they need loan at subsidized rates of interest on soft terms, they lack education, skills , capacity to save , credit- worthiness and therefore are not bankable. The experiences of several SHGs reveal that rural women are actually efficient. Availability of timely and adequate credit is essential for them to undertake any economic activity rather than credit subsidy.

In rural areas the women micro entrepreneurs continue to produce the traditional designs for local markets. Women in SHGs produce a large variety of essential products such milk, food products, village crafts and homemade snack foods. Many are engaged in retail trading of groceries and textiles. These enterprises represent a substantial supply resource for semi-urban and urban markets. SHGs are also viable organized setup to disburse micro credit to the needy entrepreneur women and encouraging their promotion of poverty alleviation activities and programmes.

WOMEN ENTREPRENEURSHIP IN INDIA

Out of total 940.98 million people in India, in the 1990s, females comprise 437.10 million representing 46.5 per cent of the total population. There are 126.48 million women workforce but as per the 1991 census, only 1,85,900 women accounting for only 4.5 per cent of the total self-employed persons in the country were recorded. As per a rough estimate the number of SSIs are expected to be 2.5 billion having 9 per cent women entrepreneurs in to it. Considering this trend, women participation in another five years was 20 % more, raising the number of women entrepreneurs to about 5,00,000. Combined effect of motivational drive, preparation of information material, conducting training, creation of women industrial estates, and training of promoters and use of mass media all together is bound to accelerate the process of women entrepreneurship development. Some psycho-social factors impede the growth of women entrepreneurs are as follows:

- Poor self-image of women
- Inadequate motivation
- Discriminating treatment
- Faulty socialization
- Role conflict
- Cultural values
- Lack of courage and self-confidence
- Inadequate encouragement
- Lack of social acceptance
- Unjust social, economic and cultural system
- Lack of freedom of expression
- Afraid of failures and criticism
- Susceptible to negative attitude
- Low dignity of labour

What New Awareness has to say about it? The new Industrial Policy of the Government of India has specially highlighted the need for special entrepreneurship programmes for women entrepreneurs in the nature of product-process oriented courses – to enable them to start small-scale industries. A majority of women entrepreneurs are from the middle class families who have low technical education, less family responsibilities but desire to become entrepreneurs. This potential should be identified and tapped.

SUMMARY

The entrepreneurs provide a magical touch to an organization, whether in public or private or joint sector, in achieving speed, flexibility, innovativeness, and a strong sense of self-determination. They bring a new vision to the forefront of economic growth. The main obstructions to socio—

economic development in rural women are due to illiteracy, poverty, lack of employment opportunities, resistance to change, lack of infrastructural facilities etc. To overcome these drawbacks, an integrated and balanced development oriented policy must be channelized. Much economic growth can be recorded by providing employment opportunities and utilizing the available resources of that area. These changes can be achieved with the joint effort of the government and the rural women.

Information gap largely affects women's development. Therefore, the Non- Governmental Organizations (NGOs) and other associations can take initiatives to make women aware and motivate them towards self-employment. At the same time, individual women should also come forward to take advantage and risks in entrepreneurial sector.

REFERENCES

1. Ankerl, G., (2000). Co-existing Contemporary Civilizations: Arabo-Mulsim, Bharati, Chinese, and Western. Geneva: Inu Press.
2. Das, P., (2004). Economic liberalisation and R&D and Innovation Responses of Indian Public and Private Sector Industries. Int. J. Manag. Decision Making 5(1), pp. 76-92.
3. Draft National Policy for Rural Industrialization-A Global Initiative, Government of India, 2003.
4. Frontline, (1997) A Continuing Social Outrage', October 4 to 17, http://www.frontlineonnet.com/fl1420/14200990.htm.
5. Gartner, W.B., 'A Conceptual Framework for Describing the Phenomenon of New Venture Creation' A Cad. Manager. Rev.10 (4), pp. 696-706, 1985.
6. Gupta RC., (1983). Spread and Triumph of Indian Numerals. Indian J. Hist. Sci. 18(1),pp. 23-38.
7. Jaya, Jaitly, 'Organising the Unorganised in Kerala: Case studies of Aruvacovanta and Kodungallur' Economic and Political Weekly, Vol. XXXII, No.28 July 12-18, 1997, pp.173.
8. Kristiansen, S. 'Information, Adaptation and Survival: A Study of Small Scale Garment Carpentry Industries in Tanzania' (A paper presented at the MU-AUC conference, Mzumbe University, 2003).
9. Leibenstein, 'Allocation Efficiency V. 'X-Efficiency', American Economic Review, LVI, 3, 1966.

10. Manimala, M.J 'Founder-culture in Organisation: Its Impact on Organizational Growth, Dynamism & innovativeness', Abhigyan (Autumn 1986).

11. Murali, K. and Jhamtani, Anita, 'Entrepreneurial Characteristics of Floriculture Farmers', Indian Journal of Extension Education, IJEE Vol. XXXIX, Jan-June 2003, pp. 19-25.

12. Nkya, Estomih J., 'Institutional Barriers to Small-Scale Business Development: A Need for Flexibility in Tanzanian Tax and Regulatory System' The Journal of Entrepreneurship, Vol. 12 (1), 2003, pp. 43-71.

13. Pandit SS., (1975), A Critical Study of the Contribution of The Arya Samaj of Indian education, Ph.D. Edu., MSU 1974-2.

14. Prime PB, Kulkarni KG (2007). Economic Development in India and China: New Perspectives on Progress and Change. New Delhi

15. Sharma, Arpana, 'Impact of Prime Minister's Rozgar Yojana in Kathua District', M Phil dissertation, University of Jammu, 2003.

16. Soly, Mossy, K.'Push Motivation: Does it Matter in Venture Performance? Paper Presented at the Babson Entrepreneurship, Rearch Conference, 1977, Wellesley.

17. Soundarapandian, M., 'Development of Rural Industries-Issues and Strategies', *Kurukshetra,* November 1999.

18. Technonet Asia, 'Entrepreneurs Handbook Institute for Small Scale Industries' Singapore NISIET library 33893 (021)/Tec/84/21477, 1981.

8

Development of Women Entrepreneurship

Dr. Santosh Singh Bais

ABSTRACT

In present scenario regarding women entrepreneurship in India, we do not have the figures to show how many women's are working as a entrepreneurs and how many women enterprises are in operation either in country or in any of the states. So it is very difficult to assess the development women entrepreneurship in India. Some rough data for three states indicates that there are about 1000 women enterprises in Karnataka, 700 in Gujarat and 500 in Tamil Nadu. It will be affair generation that while women constitute about 50 per cent of our population, the proportion of enterprises set up and run by women is a fraction of 1 per cent. The study of women as a entrepreneur is of crucial importance because the economic role that women play cannot be isolated from their total well being. Every Indian housewife is an entrepreneur in her true spirit. Their role as manager of the house can be related to the basic management techniques used in the business world of a small enterprise. The purpose of this paper is to identity the factors which influence women entrepreneurs and finding out the problems faced by them in Hyderabad Karnataka Region.

Key Words: Ardhangini, Family, Finance, Marketing, Women, Growth

INTRODUCTION

The study of women as a entrepreneur is of crucial importance because the economic role that women play cannot be isolated from their total well being. In India, women constitute about 50 per cent of the population but their participation in economic activity in only 34 per cent. During the last three decades, the position of women has been developed as result of industrial revolution, technical education and awareness. Women have realized their values in the society. Women's participation in economic activities are increasing. It accelerates nation's building and economic development activities. Emancipation of women will be a dream forever unless they are made economically independent. When women enter into various entrepreneurial activities such a pickle preparation, running beauty parlors etc, they often face lack of access to credit and face lot of obstacles to establish and develop their own business. The only solution to this is to develop women entrepreneurship. Every Indian housewife is an entrepreneur in her true spirit. Their role as manager of the house can be related to the basic management techniques used in the business world of a small enterprise. The purpose of this paper is to identity the factors which influence women entrepreneurs and finding out the problems faced by them in Hyderabad Karnataka Region.

OBJECTIVES

The following are the important objectives of the study:

1. To study the socio-economic background of the women entrepreneurs;
2. To identify the factors influencing the women entrepreneurs;
3. To find out the various constraints and problems encountered by the women entrepreneurs;
4. To make suitable suggestions for the development of women entrepreneurs;

METHODOLOGY OF THE STUDY

The study used both primary and secondary data. Primary data have been collected from the women entrepreneurs in the selected areas of Hyderabad Karnataka Region (HKR) by using structured schedule. The HKR consists five districts viz., Gulbarga, Bidar, Raichur, Bellary and Koppal. A sample of 10 women entrepreneurs have been selected in each district covering the economic activities like trading, handloom weaving, oil crushing, readymade garments, rice mills, tailoring, beauty parlours, small raw materials business.

The study covered mainly major problems and constraints faced by them during the course of starting and managing their business. And also it covered the suggestions for mitigating the problems faced by the women entrepreneurs in the HKR. The problems have been categorized into seven heads i.e. Finance, production, personnel, marketing, government assistance, occupational mobility and social personal problems.

NEED FOR WOMEN ENTREPRENEURSHIP

Women have suffered the most in our country. Women involvement in economic activities is marked by low work participation rates, excessive concentration in the unorganized sector of the economy and that too in low skill jobs. There is a greater dynamism in the rate of growth of female employment. However, in rural areas, perhaps the agriculture has provided much more employment for women. The status of women in India is an illustration of a paradox. At the micro level she has equal, if not greater position in the family as '*Ardhangini*' and she is the pivot of the socio-economic fabric of the family as a '*Mother*'. The scriptures and mythologies give her even the status of the Goddess and many women are remembered even today for their freedom struggle. However, over the period, the position of women at the macro level of the society has been downgraded so much that she is the most abused person of the Indian society.

The women in India have been neglected a lot. They have not been actively involved in the mainstream of development even though women represent almost half of our country's total population, the literacy rate of women remains at the level of 54.16 per cent as against 75.85 per cent of their male counterparts as per 2001 Census at the national level. Primarily women are the means of survival of their families, but are generally unrecognized and under valued, being placed at the bottom of the pile. Ideologically as well as in practice, women are considered completely inferior to males. Thus, the inequalities inherent in our traditional social structure based on caste, community and class have a significant influence on the low status of women in different spheres. Thus, the main issue which is still being debated is the kind of strategy to be evolved for rising their status and participation in the process of development. Hence, the emergence of women as entrepreneurs in India should be seen as a resurgence of the rightfully respectable socio-economic status of women. However, a society constrained by the suppressive socio-economic status of women. However, a society constrained by the suppressive socio-economic factors cannot generate the much needed women entrepreneurs on its own.

Education in India has been the prerogative of men over the centuries. The condition has been such that women were not given required scope for education. Besides this, the existing pattern of education in the country is not geared towards installing of entrepreneurial instincts in young minds in general and women in particular. The higher levels of education too especially commerce and management education are not directed towards generating entrepreneurship. Entrepreneurship as a subject is not a part of the curricula in many universities. And vocationalization of education is probably still a dream in our country. The politicians and policy makers are always talk about introduction and development of vocational education at +2 stage and graduation level. But in many states, vocational courses are not running systematically. The Government has not taken any initiative in this regard.

Private initiative directed towards the growth of entrepreneurs as existing in U.S.A and U.K. is not wide spread in our country. Consequently, the governmental policy directions and the performance of commercial banks, financial institutions and training institutions engaged in promoting and developing the women entrepreneurship become very crucial for the country.

In the 50 years of independence, an emphasis on the socialistic pattern of the society and the role assigned to the public sector, and limited the scope for the growth of private entrepreneurship. The liberalization policy of the government has thrown open a vast area of the economy for private entrepreneurship. Under such circumstances, special efforts to develop women entrepreneurship are more keenly felt.Women entrepreneurs are 'the women or a group of women who initiate, organize and operate a business enterprise'. The Government of India can notes women entrepreneur as "an enterprise owned and controlled by a woman having a minimum financial interest of 51 per cent of the capital and giving at least 51 per cent of the employment generated in the enterprise to women". However, this has been severally criticized on the condition of giving employment to more than 50 per cent of the total workforce to women.

FACTORS INFLUENCING THE WOMEN ENTREPRENEURSHIP

The general observation and several studies reveal that two factors influence the women entrepreneurship in India, they are as follows:

Pull Factors: Pull factors imply the factors, which encourage women to become entrepreneurs. They include desire to do something new in life, need for independence, availability of finance, concessions and subsidies.

Push Factors:

Push factors are those, which compel women to become

entrepreneurs. They include financial difficulties, responsibility in the family, unfortunate family circumstances like death of the husband or father, divorce etc. However, the influence of this factor on women in becoming entrepreneurs is lower than the former factor.

Types of Women Entrepreneurs

Women entrepreneurs can be classified into four groups depending on the driving motivational factors.

1. Natural Entrepreneurs

Natural entrepreneurs are those who take business as a profession on their own either by self pre-planning or motivated through profit or money factor and also for keeping themselves busy.

2. Created Entrepreneurs

Created entrepreneurs are those, who have been encouraged and trained through specialized training programmes such as Entrepreneurship Development Programmes (EDPs) to set up independent business.

3. Forced Entrepreneurs

Forced entrepreneurs are those who are compelled b y circumstances such as the death of father or husband with responsibilities falling on them to ztake over the existing business.

4. Bename Entrepreneurs

Bename entrepreneurs are those who are acting as a façade for business of their husband or brother.

PROBLEMS OF WOMEN ENTREPRENEURS

The problems faced by women entrepreneurs have been classified as finance, production, personnel, marketing, government assistance, occupational mobility and socio-personal.

Table 8.1: Types of Problems Faced by Sample Women Entrepreneurs

Sl.No.	Type of Problems	No. of Respondents (%)
1.	Socio-personal	(83.0)
2.	Marketing	(81.0)
3.	Occupational mobility	(57.0)
4.	Govt. assistance	(61.0)
5.	Financial	(51.0)
6.	Production	(24.0)
7.	Personnel	(25.0)

Source: Primary Data

Note: 1) Figures in Parenthesis indicates percentage of total sample.

2) Total percentage exceeds 100 as some respondents cited more than one problem.

Socio-personal Problems

In Indian society, a women from her birth until death was always sheltered by a man and had no right to being independent. With changing trends, a woman has to take care of domestic commitments and childcare support yet face résistance as an entrepreneur. About 83% of the level respondents faced this type of socio-personal problems and constraints are depicted in Table 8.2

Table 8.2: Socio-personal Problems faced by the Respondents

Sl.No.	Problems	No. of Respondents	Percentage
1.	Resistance from husband/family at the time of starting enterprise	28	56.0
2.	Dual duties (face stress)	10	20.0
3.	Indifferent attitude of society	05	10.0
4.	Non-cooperation of family members	04	08.0
5.	Backbiting by others	2	04.0
6.	Others	1	02.0
	Total	**50**	**100.0**

Source: Field Survey

It is evident from Table-8.2 that about 56 per cent of the respondents faced resistance from either husband or family or both at the time of starting their respective enterprises. While majority of the respondents said that they did not face any resistance from their husbands or families. About 20 per cent of the respondents said that they face stress while playing a dual role of an entrepreneur and housewife. Of course, this type of stress is inevitable because in typical Indian settings still a women has to perform the majority, if not whole of the household work even though she may be working elsewhere. About 10 per cent of the respondents faced with negative attitude of society like male domination. Further about eight per cent of the respondents lacked support towards the family development or the entrepreneurship.

Tabl 8.3: Reasons for Occupational Mobility

Sl No.	Reasons for occupational mobility	No. of Respondents	Percentage
1.	Preference for stability/ security orientation	23	46.0
2.	The only work known to me/ traditional	6	12.0
3.	Lack of technical knowledge	7	14.0
4.	Dual duties	3	6.0
5.	Lack of support from family members	4	8.0
6.	Lack of resources	2	4.0
7.	Lack of self-confidence	5	10.0
	Total	50	100.0

Source: Field Survey

The table shows that about 46 per cent of the sample respondents cited presence for stability/security orientation as the prime reason, which inhibits women entrepreneurs from exhibiting occupational mobility. While, 14 per cent of respondents faced with lack of technical skills since the HKR has meager literacy, where as 12 per cent of the respondents expressed that the only work known tot me and it is also a traditional one to the family. Further, only 10 per cent of the respondents had low self-confidence to promote the present unit.

Table 8.4: Problems Relating Government Assistance Faced by the Respondents

Sl.No.	Problems	No. of Respondents	Percentage
1.	Harassment in Govt. Departments	24	48.0
2.	Large amount of paper formalities	13	26.0
3.	Ignorance of laws or procedures	7	14.
4.	Discrimination with women entrepreneurs	6	12.0
	Total	**50**	**100.0**

Source: Field Survey

It may be observed from Table 8.4 that about 48 per cent of the respondents feel unhappyp due to harassment of the officials and high corruptions at various levels. While 26 per cent of the respondents cited the problems of a large amount of paper formalities, where as 14 per cent had ignorance about various procedures/laws and complicated bureaucratic set up while dealing with entrepreneurial support organization. The remaining respondents opined that there is discrimination with the women entrepreneurs while getting the government assistance.

Table 8.5: Financial Problems Faced by the Respondents

Sl.No.	Problems	No. of Respondents	Percentage
1.	Insufficient financial assistance	23	46.0
2.	Problems of security and margin money	8	16.0
3.	Tight repayment schedule	11	22.0
4.	Lack of traditional financial assistance	8	16.0
	Total	**50**	**100.0**

Source: Field Survey

Table 8.5 express about financial problems faced by the women entrepreneurs in Hyderabad Karnataka Region. About 46per cent of the total respondents feel unhappy since the financial agencies are not providing loan amount either to purchase raw material or to start new unit. While about 22 per cent of the respondents expressed that the repayment schedule is in convenient. Whereas as 16 per cent of the respondents of each demanded additional financial assistance and margin money from the concerned agencies.

Table 8.6: Production Problems Faced by the Respondents

Sl.No.	Reasons	No. of Respondents	Percentage
1.	Non-availability of raw materials	16	32.0
2.	Lack of technical assistance	14	28.0
3.	Inadequate machine tools	2	4.0
4.	Power problems	11	22.0
5.	Other infrastructural problems	7	14.0
	Total	**50**	**100.0**

Source: Field Survey

The Table 8.6 portrays about the problems faced in the production process of their working units. About 32 per cent of the respondents are suffering from non-availability of raw materials at no time. The problems of frequent price rise of raw material, which results in increasing the cost of production and thereby affecting the profitability of the unit. Where as 28 per cent of the total respondents feels that lack of technical assistance due to low educational qualifications. Further, many of the units faced that power problems and also basic amenities like pucca roads, drinking water, sanitation facilities are not available to their working units, which results low production both quality and quantity.

Marketing Problems

Marketing is another area which often decides the income levels of the entrepreneur due to the ups and downs of the demand. Many of the respondents faced a number of problems pertaining to the marketing of their products/ services. The Table 8.7 portrays the marketing problems faced by the respondents. Accordingly, about 44 per cent of the respondents cited the problems of competition from the cheaper goods. Delay payments are the problems faced by 16 per cent of our sample respondents. About 14 per cent of the respondents faced with lower demand due to the availability of substitute products, and 12 per cent of the respondents paying more transport charges, since the markets are far way to their work spot in the HKR. Further only 4 per cent of the respondents cited their inability to publicize their products due to meager financial resources.

Table 8.7: Marketing Problems Faced by the Respondents

Sl.No.	Reasons	No. of Respondents	Percentage
1.	Competition from cheaper goods	22	44.0
2.	Availability of substitute goods	7	14.0
3.	Long distance to the market	6	12.0
4.	Lack of information on changing markets	5	10.0
5.	Delay payments	8	16.0
6.	Inadequate publicity	2	4.0
	Total	50	100.0

Source: Field Survey

LOW MOBILITY PROBLEMS (OTHER PROBLEMS)

Travelling from one place to another is a problem to women entrepreneurship. Women on their own find it difficult to et accommodation in smaller town, since a single women asking for a room is still looked upon with suspicion. Officials harass many of the women, as women are believed to be less able to go through complicated court proceedings.

The foregoing discussions reveals that promotion of women entrepreneurship is far behind due to lack of financial assistance, family and community support ignorance of the opportunities, lack of motivation, shyness, inhibitions, preference for the traditional occupations etc. However, suggestions are mentioned for the growth and development of the women entrepreneurship in HKR.

As regards overcoming of the initial resistance from husband/family members at the time of start up of the enterprise the prospective women entrepreneurs are advised to maintain their cool and keep on convincing them in a positive ways regarding the usefulness of setting up of an enterprise.

The entrepreneurs should improve the quality through different techniques and acquire better skills in order to face competition. Personal contacts should be established with large number of people with a view to exploiting the mediate ship in the market and to avoid the delay payments and to improve the publicity of their products.

SUGGESTIONS

Women becoming entrepreneurs in India is still very difficult, as our patriarchal society stipulates unfavorable values for women. The experience accumulated from the study suggests focusing on the following recommendations to do away with the odds the women entrepreneurs face:

1. In addition to different financial organizations arranging special loan fund for women entrepreneurs, separate financial institutions have to be formed for women.
2. Loan should be on easy terms and interest rate must be lower for women than for usual commercial loans.
3. Assistance has to be provided to women entrepreneurs to procure raw materials.
4. Women should be advised on various issues of women entrepreneurship development and be given access to information.
5. Separate outlets may be created in all the district headquarters and other important public places where products of women entrepreneurs will be sold.
6. Government must build godowns to preserve the goods produced by women entrepreneurs.
7. Prioritized loans must be provided to women entrepreneurs to increase the production of unusual goods.
8. Women must be given institutional help to make and evaluate projects.
9. Women entrepreneurs must be motivated so that professionalism can grow among them to develop a sense of ownership.

10. They need to be cordially helped by all friends and relatives.

CONCLUSION

The saving entrepreneurs are born and not made has little sense today. A host of evidences shows that they are successfully made. In order to make women entrepreneurship movement, a success, government and non-governmental agencies have to play a vital role. There is an acute need to re-orient several things right from the grassroots level viz., increasing the number of vocational course exclusively for women, including entrepreneurship studies in commerce and management syllabi etc.

Women entrepreneurs in backward areas need special assistance and incentives from the government and financial institutions. The government shall set up[marketing agencies to ensure the timely marketing of the goods produced by women entrepreneurs. Women entrepreneurs have already created a positive trend in India through their knowledge, skill, capital and diligence. They are contributing to family, society and state withstanding multifarious problems. It is the immediate duty of all of us to work out more and vigorous strategies to eradicate all problems that impede the spread of women entrepreneurship in India. As a result such measures are reported to have tremendous positive impact on the households since there is a need to promote women entrepreneurship in the backward areas like Hyderabad Karnataka.

REFERENCES

1. Vasanthh Desai, *Entrepreneurial Development*, Himalaya Publishing House, Bombay.
2. Sarvate Dilip M., *Entrepreneurial Development—Concepts and Practices*, Everest Publishing House, Pune.
3. Jose Paul, N., Ajith Kumar and Paul T, Mampilly, *Entrepreneurship Development*, Himalaya Publishign House, Bombay.
4. L.S.Buxi, "Status of Women in India", *Yojana,* Vol.33, 1989, pp.6-8.

5. N.Kamaraju Pantulu and C. Swaralyalaskhi, *Development of Women Entrepreneurship in India*: Problems and Prospects, *The Indian Journal of Commerce*, Vol No. 193, December 19979.

6. Manimekalal, N., Nature and Characteristics of Women Entrepreneurship in India, By P. Soundarpandyan, Women Entrepreneurship Issues and Strategic.

7. Anitha H.S. and Lasmishaa A.S., "Women Entrepreneurship in India", *Southern Economist*, Vol. 38, June 15, 1999.

8. Dhameja, S.K., *Women Entrepreneurs*, Deep and Deep Publishing, New Delhi.

9

Problems and Prospects of Women Entrepreneurship

Dr. Kallinath S Patil
Dr. Santosh Singh Bais

ABSTRACT

The job market scenario in the country will continue to haunt millions of educated and uneducated. Supply will outstrip demand for ages to come. When such is the demand-supply situation, one route that many find rewarding, though there are many hurdles to be overcome is "Entrepreneurship". A large number of men and women around the world have set up and managed their own business. Entrepreneurship is not new to Indian women. Today women are entering in the field of business in increasing numbers and they do so to face many tangible obstacle. Despite numerous barriers they demonstrate a strong determination to succeed. Women have proved themselves very successful entrepreneurs by engaging in one or two income generating ventures with the confines of their family. They contribute in bringing prosperity to themselves, their family members and to the economy in general. Women owned businesses are becoming increasingly important in the economies of almost all countries. In our country also women are entering into the entrepreneurial career in a big way. At present about 7 per cent of the total enterprises in the country are being run by women. The present paper attempts to highlights the problems faced by the women entrepreneurs in India in general and Belleary district in particular.

Key Words: Development, Problems, Women, Successful, Cultural

INTRODUCTION

"When women moves forward the family moves, the village moves and the nation moves".

Pandit Jawaharlal Nehru.

Women were made to work, that sentence should be taken literally, not in the metaphorical sense that derives everyday weepies on television. "You are women", the not-so-subtle message in such programmes goes, "and it is your lot to suffer, be discriminated against and abused, and go through it all with the stoicism of a Zen monk (fine, some fears are allowed)", women to repeat, were made to work. In all but most strenuous of tasks, where they are at biological disadvantage, they acquit themselves better than their male counterparts.

Consider childbirth by early twenties, a woman is physically and mentally equipped to be a mother. Surely that has some bearing on why 22-year old woman MBA from any business school is few times as matures as her male batch mate who is still a bit of a boy. In any organization that believes in equal opportunities, the former would be one the fast track to growth and the latter, on the not-so-fast one. Even after making allowances for a 12-18 months maternity break, the woman would ahead. That many not have been the case in corporate India. Thus far (except in few companies such as ICICI Bank), but there are signs that things are slowly changing.

Today women are entering in the field of business in increasing numbers and they do so to face many tangible obstacle. Despite numerous barriers they demonstrate a strong determination to succeed. Women have proved themselves very successful entrepreneurs by engaging in one or two income generating ventures with the confines of their family. They contribute in bringing prosperity to themselves, their family members and to the economy in general. Women owned businesses are becoming increasingly important in the economies of almost all countries. In our country also women are entering into the entrepreneurial career in a big way. At present about 7 per cent of the total enterprises in the country are being run by women.

The need to conduct this study specifically of women's business ownership is based on the proposition that women problems some of which are in addition to or different from those met by men in starting and running business. In order to find out the problems and constraints being faced by business women, their managerial capabilities and training needs this study was taken up.

The present chapter makes an emphasize on the following significant factors of women entrepreneurs:

- To analyze the role of women as entrepreneur and identify the various avenues for women entrepreneurship.
- To study the general profile of women entrepreneurs and their enterprises.
- To find out the problems and constraints being faced by these business women.
- To find out the managerial capabilities of women entrepreneurs and their training needs.
- To seek the opinion of respondents regarding certain issues related to women entrepreneurship.

METHODOLOGY

Since the study was basically of a descriptive nature, the research instrument for data collection was the interview schedule. The respondents and the interview schedule were administered personally. A sample of 50 women entrepreneurs was taken according to stratified random sampling technique. The collected data was tabulated and analyzed for drawing the inferences. Due to descriptive nature of the study, statistical hypothesis were not formulated. The analysis in the study was carried out using simple statistical techniques. Inter variables relationships have been established wherever possible by carrying out cross tabulation of the available data. Primary data collected through the questionnaire is analyzed with the use of simple percentage and weighted average methods.

REVIEW OF LITERATURE

Issues related to women have attracting attention in recent years especially in the contest of social change and economic development. A number of studies have been carried out in the area. A review is made of some of the important works.

One of the major work done in the area of women and development is the book on "Women and social policy", written by Constantia Safilios Rothschild (1974) she has beautifully presented the theoretical background of social policy related to women.

In a study of "Jamanalal Bajaj Institute of Management studies" University of Mumbai 1976, an effort has been made to study the social and business implications of women managers entering the business scheme in India.

Lalitha devi in her study (1982) has tried to show that employment percentage against age, education, family type, place of residence plays a crucial role in raising the status of women.

Study conducted by Rajasthan entrepreneurs in 1983 brings out the point that women are equally effective as men in business industry·

Dr. Anali Mehta has made a study on "Women entrepreneurship in Gujarat" (1993). According to her study the women entrepreneurs appreciated the training programmes conducted by centre for entrepreneurship development (CED) but were little unhappy about the lack of substantial follow up action.

A research study (1993) in USA found that banks and financial institutions historically viewed that women entrepreneur as more doubtful propositions than men often discriminating subtly or overtly in bending practices.

A research study entitled "Entrepreneurial competition and gender wise variations" (1994) discussed the concept of entrepreneurial competencies as determinants of entrepreneurial development. The finding conclusively that gender therefore may not be the determinant of competence levels in twin entrepreneur success.

An exploratory research study on "women entrepreneurs in transition (1994) identified five transitions in women entrepreneurs based on analysis of 150 cases of women entrepreneurs in India despite predicting the future trends.

An empirical study on "emerging profile of small women entrepreneurs–cum–managers in India a case study" revealed that women entrepreneurs in India engaged in died variety of non-traditional business activities are well equipped with education and experience and are highly motivated to their business independently and are prepared to face any challenge. They are fully involved in the business so as to gain and enhance economic and social status.

Dr. Hanumant Yadav, in his research paper "Problem of Women Entrepreneurship in Eastern Madhya Pradesh" (1998) revealed that the paucity of funds is the cruse of all the problems. If it is solved half of the major problems are solved.

NEED FOR THE STUDY

It is evident from the preceding brief review of literature that issues related to women have been attracting attention in recent years especially in the context of social and economic development. Therefore, on account of their importance, studies on women entrepreneurship have been carried out (or) are in the process in almost every economy. A few studies that are available are mostly surveys of economic aspects and of problems of running the industrial units. Many of these are also related or conducted in metropolitan or urban areas. There are no previous studies that constraints data on prospect of women entrepreneurship in a backward area like Bellary District in Karnataka has been undertaken. Therefore, it has incited us to undertake the study.

LIMITATION OF THE STUDY

The study is not free from the certain limitations. This study is limited only to women entrepreneurs of Bellary

District of Karnataka, has been chosen for the purpose of the study due to time and resource constraint.

As the questionnaire covers various aspects of the study, the respondents may not be able to answer certain questions, many of them have given poor response to questionnaire it is very difficult to present the exact information from their memory.

Conclusion and projection in some cases are to be based on the researcher's own judgment. Therefore, the personal limitations of the researcher need special mention.

NEED FOR WOMEN ENTREPRENEURSHIP

The emergence of women entrepreneurs in a society depends to a great extent on the economic, religious, cultural, social, psychological and other factors. Hence, the emergence of women as entrepreneurs in India should be seen as a resurgence of the rightfully respectable socio-economic status of women. However, a society constrained by suppressive socio-economic factors cannot generate the much needed women entrepreneurs on its own. The women were not given regained scope for education in the country. The private initiatives directed towards the growth of entrepreneurs as existing in USA and in UK are not wide spread in our country. Moreover, women have become the integral part of the industrialized society.

Women are expected to come out from tradition by taking up self employment ventures. The liberalization policy of the government has thrown-up to open a vast area of the economy for private entrepreneurship under such circumstances special efforts to develop women entrepreneurship is keenly felt. A very few women entrepreneurs have had successful in their venture having different background in the Indian corporate world they are Ekta Kapoor (creative director of Balaji Tlifilms), Kiran Mazumadar Shaw (founder and director of Biocon Groups), Anu Aga (chairperson, Thermax), Lalita Gupte (Joint M.D ICICI Bank), Renu Karnad (Executive Director HDFC), Naina Kidwailal (Deputy CEO, HSBC) etc.

SOCIO-ECONOMIC CONDITIONS OF WOMEN ENTREPRENEURS

An entrepreneur's works as an investor, promoter, organizer, manager, coordinator and also a capitalized she takes decisions with regard to work inside the house, the some would be extended in the work place. Findings of the study under taken by Shanta Kholi Chandra reveals that socio-economic factor are affecting the women entrepreneurs. In her study majorities of women entrepreneurs are young, and do not belong to business families. Marital status and family bindings in majority of the cases did not interfere significant in continuing the enterprise.

PERIOD OF ESTABLISHMENT

The numbers of enterprises established by women entrepreneurs in Bellary district are very less being it is a backward area, less literacy rate, and are also not financially sound, very few women entrepreneurs are there. Even among them very few women entrepreneurs are successful.

Table 9.1: Number of Enterprises Established by Women Entrepreneurs

Sl. No.	Year of establishment	Total	
		No. of women entrepreneurs	Percentage
1.	Below 1970	2	8
2.	1970 – 1980	1	4
3.	1980-1990	2	8
4.	1990-2000	15	60
5.	2000-2001	2	8
6.	2001-2002	3	12
	Total	**25**	**100**

Source: Field investigation

The critical evaluation of the above table reveals that, there is a greater variation among male and female entrepreneurs towards the establishment of entrepreneurs towards the establishment of enterprises. Not even 8 per cent has been covered towards enterprises established by women enterprises in Bellary district in 2000-2001.

Table 9.2: Age Wise Classification of Respondents

Sl. No.	Age	Total	
		No. of women entrepreneurs	Percentage
1.	10-20	2	8
2.	20-30	11	44
3.	30-40	7	28
4.	40-50	2	8
5.	50-60	2	8
6.	Above – 60	1	4
	Total	**25**	**100**

Source: Field investigation

It can be evident from the above table-9.2 out of the 11 women entrepreneurs in Bellary district of the women entrepreneurs belong to the age group of 20-30 years, in second position 28 per cent women entrepreneurs belong to 30-40 age groups in study area. In third position 8 per cent of women entrepreneurs belong to below 20 years age group and same per cent of women entrepreneurs were also belonged to 40-50 age groups and 50-60 age groups. Most of the women entrepreneurs are middle age; this group attains some maturity to settle in the field of entrepreneurship.

Table9.3: Level of Education

Sl. No.	Education level	Total	
		No. of women entrepreneurs	Percentage
1.	Illiteracy	3	12
2.	1-10	13	52
3.	10-12	2	8
4.	12-15	4	16
5.	15-17	1	4
6.	Professional	2	8
	Total	**25**	**100**

Source: Field investigation

It is clear from the above table-9.3 education wise analysis shows that most of the women entrepreneurs are in below graduation level. Being the district is in backward region even some women entrepreneurs are there with no education. Some women entrepreneurs are expert in technical field. In Bellary district majority of the women are in High School Level (52%) and in the case of second place is Degree level (16%) and third place is illiteracy of women entrepreneurs i.e., (12%).

Table 9.4: Religion and Caste Wise Distribution

Sl.No.	Caste	Total	
		No. of women entrepreneurs	Percentage
1.	Scheduled caste	3	12
2.	Scheduled tribe	1	4
3.	Backward caste	17	68
4.	Other caste	4	16
	Total	25	100

Source: Field investigation

Above table-9.4 reveals that among the women entrepreneurs covered by the sample study are belonged to different casts, caste and religion has also placed a significant role in entrepreneurship development. 68 per cent of sample sizes are belonged to backward caste, SC and ST women entrepreneurs are few in numbers i.e., 12 per cent and 4 per cent respectively.

Table 9.5: Religion Wise Distribution

Sl. No.	Religion	Total	
		No. of women entrepreneurs	Percentage
1.	Hindu	23	92
2.	Muslim	2	8
3.	Christian -	–	–
4.	Others	–	–
	Total	25	100

Source: Field investigation

It is clear from the above table that most of the women entrepreneurs belong to other backward classes category and non-reserved class. Among the women entrepreneurs covered by the sample study 92 per cent were belonged to Hindu in Bellary district and rest of 8 per cent belonged to Muslims.

Table 9.6: Marital status

Sl. No.	Particulars	Total	
		No. of women entrepreneurs	Percentage
1.	Unmarried	4	16
2.	Married	21	84
3.	Windows	–	–
	Total	**25**	**100**

Source: Field investigation

Marital status of women entrepreneurs will also have an influence towards the success of enterprise. It is clear from the above table that 16 per cent women entrepreneurs are unmarried and remaining 84 per cent women entrepreneurs in Bellary district were married. They are all running the enterprise with the help of their family members.

Table 9.7: Type of Family

Sl. No.	Family type	Total	
		No. of women entrepreneurs	Percentage
1.	Joint family	7	28
2.	Nuclear family	18	72
	Total	25	100

Source: Field investigation

Type of family will play a significant role in the development of women entrepreneurs. It is clear from the above table that majority of women entrepreneurs are living in nuclear family and they are managing the enterprises very easily. Table 9.7 shows that it shows that 72 per cent of the women entrepreneurs in Bellary district belong to nuclear family and rest of respondents belonged to joint family. It indicates that to manage the business successfully nuclear family environment is more favourable for the women entrepreneurs.

Table 9.8: Family Background

Sl. No.	Family Background	Total	
		No. of women entrepreneurs	Percentage
1.	Agriculture	12	48
2.	Business	9	36
3.	Industry	1	4
4.	Services	2	8
5.	Others	1	4
	Total	**25**	**100**

Source: Field investigation

The family background of women entrepreneurs will play an important role for the development of women entrepreneurship. It is clear from the above table that most of the family members of the women entrepreneurs are from the agriculture background. In Bellary district it stood at 48 per cent. It emphasizes the fact that a family background of agriculture experience influence to a greater degree in taking to entrepreneurship as a career. Business environment in the family, encouragement and support from the family members, and at some times situational forces all has combined for the women entrepreneurs in setting up of an enterprise.

Table 9.9: Type of the Enterprise

Sl. No.	Type of enterprise	Total	
		No. of women entrepreneurs	Percentage
1.	Manufacturing	16	64
2.	Job working	2	8
3.	Servicing	4	16
4.	Assembling	1	4
5.	Sub-contracting	2	8
	Total	**25**	**100**

Source: Field investigation

A study has also been carried out to know about the type of the enterprise, which the women entrepreneurs are carrying out. The above table reveals that most of the women entrepreneurs were in manufacturing sector in Bellary district (64%). Servicing here refers being in the business of Beauty parlor, tailoring, hotels, computer centre etc. In second place is servicing sector in Bellary district with 16 per cent of sample group.

Table 9.10: Age of the Enterprise

Sl. No.	Period of establishment	Total	
		No. of women entrepreneurs	Percentage
1.	1-5	14	56
2.	5-10	7	28
3.	10-15	2	8
4.	Above 15	2	8
	Total	**25**	**100**

Source: Field investigation

The critical evaluation of above table portraits that most of the enterprises i.e., 56 per cent of sample size are having age of the enterprise in between 1-5 years of age and 28 per cent are in between 5-10 years of age.

Table 9.11: Ownership of the Firm

Sl. No.	Type of enterprises	Total	
		No. of women entrepreneurs	Percentage
1.	Proprietorship	16	64
2.	Partnership	6	24
3.	Co-operatives	1	4
4.	Private limited	1	4
5.	Public limited	1	4
6.	Others	–	0
	Total	25	100

Source: Field investigation

The above table indicates that the majority of units are sole proprietorship units. A sole trader is one who carries as the business by herself and sharing profit and losses individually and bearing unlimited liabilities, some are the units were found in private limited and public limited company and co-operative form of organization in the survey taken from the women entrepreneurs of Bellary district.

Table 9.12: Location of the Entrepreneurs

Sl. No.	Location of the entrepreneurs	Total	
		No. of women entrepreneurs	Percentage
1.	Urban	16	64
2.	Semi-urban	4	16
3.	Rural	5	20
	Total	**25**	**100**

Source: Field Investigation

It is clear from the above table that most of the women entrepreneurs belong to the urban area (64%). It shows the higher awareness among the women of the urban area towards entrepreneurship. There are so many factors for the less awareness in rural areas, for example lack of education, lack of proper guidance, lack of required information about the business, facilities and services available, orthodox social with religious environment working as subsidiary in the agriculture etc.

Table 9.13: Period of Working Days

Sl. No.	Period of working days	Total	
		No. of women entrepreneurs	Percentage
1.	Regular	19	76
2.	Seasonal	6	24
	Total	**25**	**100**

Source: Field investigation

There are certain industries where it works in only seasonal periods for example in case of papad industries, the season is between December–May during that period only the processing of papad industry takes place. It is evident from the above table that majority of the units i.e., 76 per cent were regular in nature. Regular units such as tailoring, beauty parlour, computer center, hotel, embroidering etc., and rest of 24 per cent carry their business on seasonal basis.

Table 9.14: Size of Total Investment

Sl. No.	Size of investment (in ₹)	Total	
		No. of women entrepreneurs	Percentage
1.	1,000 to 10,000	14	56
2.	10,000 to 50,000	7	28
3.	50,000 to 1,00,000	2	8
4.	1,00,000 to 5,00,000	1	4
5.	Above 5,00,000	1	4
	Total	**25**	**100**

Source: Field investigation

The above table shows that almost 92 per cent of the units are having an investment of below ₹1 lakh, being very backward region women were not well equipped for which women entrepreneurs will start small scale industries, in case of tailoring, embroidering, hotel, papad industries the investment required is less. Even in Xerox centers and beauty parlour initial investment is less. This shows the initial capacity and the standard of women entrepreneurs in Bellary district was very poor.

Table 9.15: Type of Women Entrepreneurs in Bellary District

Sl. No.	Types of work	Total	
		No. of women entrepreneurs	Percentage
1.	Tailoring	7	28
2.	Beauty parlour	2	8
3.	Hand pumps	1	4
4.	Garments	2	8
5.	Ophthalmologist/clinic	1	4
6.	Computer	1	4
7.	Papad industry	2	8
8.	Self employment	3	12
9.	Hotel	1	4
10.	Department store	1	4

(Contd...)

11.	Painting and embroidering	1	4
12.	General fancy	–	–
13.	Bangle store	1	4
14.	Agarbatti	–	–
15.	Bakery	1	4
16.	Herbal production	–	–
17.	Beauty care	1	4
18.	Flour mill	–	–
	Total	**25**	**100**

Source: Field investigation

The areas selected by women entrepreneurs toward their venture differ from women to women and also from place to place moreover, it depends upon the financial capacity, educational background etc. It shows that the women are not economically sound and are not well educated. They even do not possess the technical skills. As Bellary district is a backward district. 28 per cent of sample size is engaged in tailoring and 1per cent of sample group are engaged in garment, hotel and agarbatti business etc.

Table 9.16: Training and Experience of Women Entrepreneurs

Sl. No.	Trained/untrained women entrepreneurs	Total	
		No.of women entrepreneurs	Percentage
1.	Trained women entrepreneurs	23	92
2.	Untrained women entrepreneurs	2	8
	Total	**25**	**100**

Source: Field Investigation

The above table shows that more percentage of women entrepreneurs has undergone training for the women entrepreneurs in Bellary district as given by District Industries Centre (DIC) and Syndicate Institute of Rural Development (SIRD) to start. Beauty parlour, computer centres, tailoring and other business. 92 per cent of sample size undergone training and only 8 per cent of sample size are untrained.

Influencing Factors of Women Entrepreneurs

Motivational or influencing factor plays a predominant role in starting the enterprise. There may be internal factors and external factors which motivate women entrepreneurs to start business. External factors are government, societies, family members, relatives and friends.

Each respondent was asked to pick and rank them according to the importance she attached to each of the reasons mentioned by her is shown in below table.

Table 9.17: Source of Media About This Business

Sl. No.	Sources of media about this business	Total	
		No. of women entrepreneurs	Percentage
1.	Government	6	24
2.	Societies	2	8
3.	Electric media	1	4
4.	Print medias	1	4
5.	Friends and relatives	14	56
6.	Others	2	8
	Total	**25**	**100**

Source: Field investigation

Most of the women entrepreneurs selected for the study 58 per cent of sample size agreed that they have got sufficient support and co-operation from their family whether they belong to nuclear family or joint family. This indicates the importance of influencing factor of family co-operation for the development of women entrepreneurship.

Government acquires second importance with the weighted score of 24 points in Bellary district. Others ranked third with the weighted score in Bellary district.

An attempt has also been made in this regard by examining the important internal motivational factor influencing on women to establish enterprise viz. professional, by birth, economic profit, to be economically independent, to do something to till time, it's my hobbies and to do social service.

Table 9.18: Reason for Starring this Business

Sl. No.	Reasons for this business	Total	
		No. of women entrepreneurs	Percentage
1.	Professional	3	12
2.	By birth	1	4
3.	Earning profit	11	44
4.	To be economical independent	2	8
5.	To do something worth	1	4
6.	It's my hobbies	1	4
7.	To do social service	5	20
	Total	**25**	**100**

Source: Field investigation

The above table indicates that the prominent factors which are encouraged the women entrepreneurs to start the enterprise in Bellary district. "Economic profit" has been the prime motivation or influencing factor which acquires to top most importance with the weighted score of 44 in Bellary district.

Utilization of capital resources of the family stood second position. As explained earlier, family will play a predominant role in influencing the women entrepreneurs, some women entrepreneurs want to fulfill their own ambition. This will also play an influencing factor for staring the enterprise.

The third influencing factor which makes women entrepreneurs to start the enterprise is awareness about the idea of starting the enterprise.

Source of awareness for the largest single group were advice from friends and relatives with the weighted score of 56 points, the next most important reason was visit to similar DIC in the district with the weighted score of 24 points and others in a similar unit ranked as third reason for starting a industrial.

Table 9.19: Source of Information

Sl. No.	Come to know about this business	Total	
		No. of women entrepreneurs	Percentage
1.	Government	6	24
2.	Societies	1	4
3.	Electronic medias	1	4
4.	Print medias	1	4
5.	Friends and relatives	14	56
6.	Others	2	8
	Total	**25**	**100**

Source: Field investigation

Location Factors

In an attempt to study the location factors that influence the women entrepreneurs in starting up their venture. Severn factors were identified by 25 women entrepreneurs in Bellary district and each women entrepreneurs was asked to indicate three factors that were most encouraging to her in the order of priority in starting her unit.

Table 9.20: Locational Factors in Bellary District

Sl. No.	Kind of assistance/ help you require	Total	
		No. of women entrepreneurs	Percentage
1.	Incentive from government	–	–
2.	Subsidized loan	13	52
3.	Interest free loan	2	8
4.	Raw material supply at concessional rate	1	4
5.	Purchase of finished product by government	1	4
6.	Easy finance/loans on bank and financial institution	4	16
7.	Protection of small women entrepreneurs	4	16
	Total	**25**	**100**

Source: Field investigation

Subsidized loans were perceived as the most encouraging factor among 13 entrepreneurs.The next most encouraging factor was protection of small women entrepreneurs, followed by easy finance/loans by bank and financial institutions.

PROBLEMS IN WOMEN ENTREPRENEURS

The new thrust given to the process of economic development of the country by the new dynamic leadership has created an all round enthusiasm and the new slogan of "March towards the 21st century" has gained popularity, but in this new enthusiasm towards the economic development of the country is not given much attention as required and that sector is women entrepreneurs.

The biggest problem against a women entrepreneur is that she is a women. Its means that the attitude of society towards women and constraints in which she has to live and works is quite address. Women are still suffering from male reservations. These reservations create difficulties and problems at all level i.e., family support, training, financial licensing and marketing women in non-urban areas have to suffer still further.

The following table shows the factors that inhibited women entrepreneurs or the problems faced by women entrepreneurs in the process of starting the unit in Bellary district.

Table9.21: Discoursing Factors in Bellary District

Sl. No.	Problems/discouraging factor	Total	
		No. of women entrepreneurs	Percentage
1.	Competition	14	57
2.	Price fluctuation	3	12
3.	Irregular supply of raw materials	2	9
4.	Storage	–	–
5.	Bargaining	1	2
6.	Fluctuation in demand	2	9
7.	Lack of experience	1	3
8.	Lack of technical know how	1	6
9.	Capital shortage	1	2
	Total	**25**	**100**

Source: Field investigation

From the above table it can be noted that competition came out as the most influencing factor by the entire respondent (25 respondents in Bellary district) concerned.

The second highest problem by women entrepreneurs is price fluctuation in district. Third highest problem faced by women entrepreneurs in Bellary district, is irregularly supply of raw materials and fluctuation in demand for certain industries such as cloths, beauty creams, electricity facility and raw materials is important to produce the ultimate product.

Another important problem face by women entrepreneurs was in relation to lack of technical know how, it plays very predominant role in the development of woman entrepreneurs and also enterprise.

Even from the above table it can be observed that "competition was biggest problem faced by women entrepreneurs, it might be either from male entrepreneurs or from fellow entrepreneurs. Women entrepreneurs cited interest to do businesses as the main reason behind their planning into the entrepreneur's world. Some of these said that business was in their blood and they have a love for business profession. The other problems faced by women entrepreneurs are as follows:

- Lack of suitable and appropriate environment for promotion of entrepreneurship.
- Lack of confidence to start their venture
- Social pressure and attitude of debuting a women's capability
- Inadequate involvement of financial and other agencies to assist women to tackle problems that of finance etc.

CONCLUSION

Finally it can be concluded that, the women entrepreneurs must accept all the challenges and should overcome with her enthusiasm and confidence in herself. In a study made in

Bellary district most of the women entrepreneurs are managing their business simply without any urge to expand, develop or grow the enterprise, they are managing business in a traditional way since a long time, they do not even bother to change their technology of production and even the way of marketing of the product. They are satisfied only with their existing system, such an attitude on the part of any entrepreneurs is not desirable. The business world moving ahead in all aspects in the midst of cut throughout competition at national and international level.

REFERENCES

1. Airken Huge, J. *"Explorations in Enterprise"* Ed. Harward University Press, Cambridge, 1965, p.46.
2. Anitha Sharma, *"Modernization and Station of Working Women in India,"*, Mittal publications, New Delhi, 1990.
3. Bhanushah, S.G. *"Entrepreneurship Development"*, Himalaya Publishing House, 1981, Bombay.
4. Chandra Shantha Kohli, *"Development of Women in India,"* Shakti Books, Delhi.
5. Devendra *"Status and Position of Women in India"*, Shakti Books, Delhi.
6. Gosavi, M. S. *"Business Education and Entrepreneurs Development"*, Ed. Gokhale Education Society's Publication, Nasik, 1986.
7. Gupta Ashish *"Indian Entrepreneurs Culture"*. Vishwas Prakasha, U. K., 1994.
8. Anjali Metha, *" A Study an Women Entrepreneurs in Gujarat"*, Summary Published in Times of India," Ahmedabad, 8 December, 1993.
9. Patel, V. G., *"Entrepreneurs Are Not Born"*, *Economic Times*, December 21, August, 1991.
10. Tinani Madan, *"Women Entrepreneurs"*,—An Article Published in the *Economic times"*, 10th April 1998.

10

Some Successful Women Entrepreneurs in India

Dr. Pandit C. Bilamge
Dr. Santosh Singh Bais

ABSTRACT

Recently, the role of women in the Indian society has changed considerably. Women today are no longer confined to the kitchen and the four walls of the house. But they have been actively participating in every economic activity and successfully proving that they can excel in any activity. There are many successful women entrepreneurs, educationists, professionals, scientists, economists, etc. Women in our country constitute 48.15 per cent of the total population, as per census 2001. Therefore, development of the Indian economy is not possible without the participation of women who constitute a large segment of the society. Like both hands are necessary to do any work properly, it is essential that men and women are given equal oppurtunities to work, so that they can increase their family income in particular and the country's income in general. During the last two decades, Indian women have entered the field of entrepreneurship in greatly increasing numbers. With the emergence and growth of their businesses, they have contributed to the global economy and to their surrounding communities. The routes women have followed to take leadership roles in business are varied. Yet, most women business owners have overcome or worked to avoid obstacles and challenges in creating their businesses. The presence of women in the workplace driving small and entrepreneurial organizations creates a tremendous impact on employment and business environments.

INTRODUCTION

Indian women business owners are changing the face of businesses of today, both literally and figuratively. The dynamic growth and expansion of women-owned businesses is one of the defining trends of the past decade, and all indications are that it will continue unabated. For more than a decade, the number of women-owned businesses have grown at one-and-a-half to two times the rate of all businesses. Even more important, the expansion in revenues and employment has far exceeded the growth in numbers.

The result of these trends is that women-owned businesses span the entire range of business life cycle and business success, whether the measuring stick is revenue, employment or longevity. This strengthens the view that all governmental programmes and policies should target at strengthening women's entrepreneurship in their native lands. The world is moving at a fast pace women entrepreneurs will not left behind. Yet, they need the help of the communications and information systems. As an entrepreneur a women is competing with a male entrepreneur's manager and has to be on an equal footing with him. The position of the women entrepreneur is vibrant and she is eager to make a place for herself in the emerging industrial society not only in India but also in the world.

DEVELOPMENT OF WOMEN ENTREPRENEURSHIP IN INDIA

Women have proved themselves very successful entrepreneurs by engaging in one or two income generating ventures within the confines of their homes. The opportunity for developing the home based small scale entrepreneurship has become more due to increased level of education among women. There is an urgent need to promote avenues for these women to take up entrepreneurship in the 21st century in order to exploit their talents which otherwise go waste. Certain measures which will help in the development of entrepreneurship among women are as follows

- Motivation of women to become economically independent and take up the challenge of starting their own business;
- Inculcation of personality traits like determination and strong will power;
- Awareness and education about policy and programmes among women;
- Well equipped training and resource centres to meet the needs of women entrepreneurs;
- Complete family support;
- Involvement of all promotional agencies in providing support in the areas of infrastructure, finance, raw materials, marketing and human resource management;
- Access to saving and credit;

Regardless of the nature of enterprise, which may be on individual or group basis, the women entrepreneur should have an organizational backing-an organization in which she is an equal partner along with other women and which can lend it support in terms of financial and non-financial services including credit, training, business counseling etc. besides being a forum for inter-support and collective action.

It is appropriate to encourage women for entrepreneurial activity with their 'empowerment' as the goal, the developmental professionals in their enthusiastic must not ignore the main subjects i.e. the women themselves, for she already has definite functions to perform in the family sphere.

As already mentioned, in most developing countries, women are still struggling against many obstacles in built in their social status. On the other hand, the proportion of educated and skilled women in total unemployment is increasing. These conditions are changing due to changing economic norms, modernization and technology up gradation, development of trade and have led then towards self employment/ entrepreneurship. Yet, intensive efforts/ allocations involved in developing women of lower concentrate on traditional products like food and garments. This in the long run, creates unhealthy competition because of large number of women being in the same business.

Leading women to entrepreneurship and the right business opportunity, therefore, demands a systematic and scientific approaches. Women EDPs must cover all aspects not only for establishment and running of enterprise but also for development of their entrepreneurial and managerial competencies. At present in India, almost all states are involved in women EDPs and self employment development programmes supporting facilities like infrastructure and finance are quite favourable.

NEEDS OF WOMEN ENTREPRENEURS IN INDIA

- More and better access to finance/credit is mentioned very frequently. Give a woman 1000 rupees and she can start a business. Give her another 1000 rupees and she will be able to feed not only for her family, but for her employees as well.
- Access to business support and information, including better integration of business services.
- Training on business issues and related issues
- Better access to local and foreign markets.
- Day care centres and nurseries for children, and also for the elderly.
- Positive image-building and change in mentality amongst women, whereby women see themselves as capable achievers and build up confidence.
- Breaking through traditional patrons and structures that inhibit women's advancement.
- Role modelling of women in non-traditional business sectors to break through traditional views on men's and women's sectors.

- More involvement and participation in legislation and decision-making processes.
- Removing of any legislation which impedes women's free engagement.

SCOPE OF WOMEN ENTREPRENEURSHIP IN INDIA

The emergence of women entrepreneurs and their contribution to the national economy is quite visible in India. The number of women entrepreneurs has grown over a period of time, especially in the 1990s. Women entrepreneurs need to be lauded for their increased utilization of modern technology, increased investments, finding a niche in the export market, creating a sizeable employment for others and setting the trend for other women entrepreneurs in the organized sector.

It is estimated that women entrepreneurs presently comprise about 10 per cent of total number of entrepreneurs in India, with the per cent growing every year and if the prevailing trends continue it is likely that in another five years women will comprise 20 per cent of entrepreneurial force. With the corporate sector eager to associate and work with women owned businesses and a host of banks and non-governmental organizations keen to help them get going, there has rarely been a better time for women, with zeal and creativity, to start their own business.

SUCCESSFUL WOMEN ENTREPRENEURS

Here are few women entrepreneurs who have had successful in their venture having different backgrounds.

Ekta Kapoor

Ekta Kapoor, the daughter of a successful film star was said to be the face and brain of ***Balaji Telifilms Limited*** (BTL). In her childhood she was an avid television watcher and spent most of her free time glued to the TV. She felt guilty about letting her parents down, but was unable to do anything. The turning point in Ekta Kapoor's life came in the early 1990s when a non-resident Indian, Ketan Somayya, approach her father and requested him to make some software for the channel he wanted to start. Ekta's father asked her to take up the responsibility of making the software. Consequently, Ekta Kapoor made six pilots, of about three episodes each, at a cost of about ₹ 0.5 million. The proposed channel, however, did not fare well and had to be sold to Zee TV. BTL was set up in 1994 by her father; Mano Ya Na Mano (believe it or not) first serial was telecast in 1995. This was followed by Dhum Dhamaka (Musical explosion). The first major success came with Hum Paanch (we five), BTL came out with an initial public offer (IPO) in October 2000 to set up integrated studio in Mubmai and to buy advanced equipment. The initial years of the business were not easy for Ekta Kapoor. There were times when she used to have 5 or 6 pilots ready but none of them would get approval from the channels. People did not take her seriously. Her hard work and commitment eventually paid off, and by the early 2000s she had two highly successful serials, Kyunki Saans Bhi Kabhi Bahu Thi and Kahani Ghar Ghar Ki Ekta Kapoor believed that her initial failures contributed a lot to her success at a later stage. After her first few projects failed, she became more careful. She started watching television carefully to analyze the programmes that were successful and those that have flopped to understand the likes and dislikes of the changes in Indian television. Ekta Kapoor managed to change the concept of prime time television from 10.30 p.m. a prime time slot to 8.00 and 9.30 p.m. She paid a lot of attention to detail and monitored all aspects of BTL's serials for the first few episodes. Her unique style of naming the serials (All names started with 'K') also drew the attention of viewers. On the human resource front, Ekta Kapoor seemed to be some thing of an autocrat. She yelled at her subordinates as she believed that if she did not shout, things would not get done. She was able to succeed because:

1. She did not depend on any one channel.
2. BTL diversified risk by distributing resources between commissioned and sponsored serials.
3. The cost of production was kept under control.

4. Actors were also employed on a contractual basis which gave the producer more control over them.

She received a number of awards important are "Earnst and young entrepreneur of the year in 2001", "Corporate Excellence" from Bharat Petroleum in 2002 and "Rajiv Ghandi Award in 2002"

Kiran Mazumdar Shaw

She is India's first women brew master and the fonder director of ***Biocon Group.*** India's first lady biotech entrepreneur, she born in Bangalore educated in Bishop Cotton Girls School. Her childhood ambition was to be a doctor but when she was unable to get admission in medical college. She decided to develop career in the science of fermentation and qualified as a brew master from Melbourne. After her return to India, she worked with her father for a few years as a consultant to some breweries. She started Biocon India in 1978 in a joint venture with the Irish firm. The company was fist set up in her garage in Bangalore.

Banks and Financial institutions were wary of giving her loans as biotechnology was a new filed and was therefore considered 'high risk'. Being a women, and one with no business qualification at that, made things even more difficult. She also faced with problems recruiting people. People were reluctant to work for women entrepreneurs as they doubted their creditability. She believed in encouraging an open and supportive culture at Biocon. The company had a flat organizational structure and anybody in the organization, from the peons to the presidents, had equal access to her. She believed that motivation comes from empowerment and consequently, she encouraged her employees to challenge themselves and solve their own problems.

In the beginning of years of the business, she believed in employing more women than men in her company. But she realized that a large number of women eventually suffered to societal or family pressures and stopped working. She therefore decided to recruit on the competency parameter alone. The ratio of men and women was 1.5 : 4 in 2002. Under her leadership, Biocon grew from a small business in the garage of her house to becoming the largest biotech company in India. She won number of awards such as Rotary award for best model employer, M. Visweshariah award in 2002 for her achievement.

Arnavaj 'Anu' Aga: (Chairperson Thermax)

India has enough male industrialist and CEOs who have grown into the postion of elder statesman- Ratan Tata, Rahul Bajaj and N.R Narayana Murthy—but Anu Aga is the first women who qualify for that distinction. With her patrician features and striking cropped silver mane, the lady is a regular at industry fore, and when she talks, people listen. That's not just because Aga built the Pune based Thermax Group into a ₹ 830 Core energy and environmental engineering major. It is not because of her stated objective of "doubling turnover and trembling profits in the next three years" . it is because she speaks (and acts) from the heart. This is evident in Thermax's practice of putting aside 1 per cent of its profits for social causes and its generous contributions towards efforts to beatify Pune. And it is evident in Aga's own association that strives to provide education to children who live in slums and on the streets.

Last year, one of this magazine's writers wrote " Aga will definitely not feature in the next listing she turns 62 in September 2004 and will hand over charge as chairperson". Now, with the date of her retirement drawing close, it emerges that Aga's power was never positional (arising from the post she held); it was always personal—arising from truth, fairness, transparency and corporate ethics. That could explain why the economics graduate (she also has a PG degree from Mumbai's Tata Institute of Social science) was motivated by a letter from a concerned shareholder to put aside her grief at the death of her husband and Thermax's founder Rohinton, and focus on the ailing company. As it could, her outspoken criticism of the way the government of Gujarat handled the sectarian violence that broke out in the state in early 2002. Vipassana, a form of meditation, Aga claims, has made her stronger and helps her keep in touch with her inner voice. She said that she felt very blessed.

Kavita Hurry: (MD ING Vysya Mutual Fund)

Contrary to her name, Kavita Hurry is not a woman given to extremes. For one, balance is important to her. " life is about balance" she muses philosophically. It is a Monday, Hurry is in her 13th floor apartment in Cuffe parade, a tony down Mumbai neighboured, having taken the day off after all the excitement of an initial public offering of an ING Vysya scheme that has just closed, and she is checking on the status of her children's home work over the phone (she has two aged 13 and 10).

The lady's career is an embodiment of that balance. First, the class of MBA from Mumbai's Narsee Monee Institute of Management Studies opted to join Bank of Credit and Commerce despite juggling offers from a hotel and an advertising agency because her parents were not too comfortable with their daughter working in hospitality of advertising. Then, she opted to stay on in Mumbai when she signed on with ING. She cannot leave Mumbai as her husband was running business and kinds were in school. In several corporations that could be an issue, but she picked something like private banking where customers want long term relationships and the business, therefore, requires that you be stationary. The moderation extended to Hurry's work too. She eould rather not set any targets for the quantum of funds she manages (she currently did Rs.1800 crore). She looked at size very differently, she said that it matters but what is the point of managing Rs.4000 crore if we are not making money. She always believed that corporate customers should talk to people, actually make eye contact, and talk. She had not spent anything on advertising. She has clinched her teeth and decided to do it her way, which means a lot more.

M. K Kamala

There are many agencies which are playing a catalytic role in entrepreneurial development and one such is the Small Industrial Service Institute (SISI)". There are many young educated unemployed who knock the doors of SISI and have come up trumps in life.

M. K Kamala, the founder of ***'Panchajanya Enterprises'*** is thankful to SISI for the entrepreneurship development programme. She started her career as a stenographer and later became a manger in Pharmacy Company. She came to know about SISI and the training programmes it offered for setting up small units. She enrolled for the EDP in manufacturing chemicals in 2003. it is a one month programme and it gave a lot of information to her, particularly about phenyl production. There was one week of practical training in manufacturing process. Soon after, they set up the company to manufacture cleaning products. The first year, they had to face practical problems in running an industry which is highly demanding in terms of product specification. The expectations of pharmacy companies are high. They started Panchajanya Enterprises with of ₹2lakhs and now turnover is 24lakhs. She felt that by getting trained in SISI, they had generated more employment and it is satisfying.

Jayalakshmi Satish

For Jayalakshmi Satish, working as a teacher was not remunerative; hence she set up a unit of her own, having trained at SISI for manufacture of cleaning products. Her company sells cleaning products under the brand name 'Raksha' and she owns her success to SISI. She went to SISI for EDP in manufacture of cleaning products. She learnt about manufacturing, packing, marketing etc. However, after setting up the manufacturing unit, initially they had practical problems. Now they have stared manufacturing of room fresheners and they are eco-friendly.

Shri Mahila Griha Udyog Lijjat Papad (SMGULP)

The entrepreneurial success of SMGULP is noteworthy. SMGULP was a cooperative system in which women over the age of 18 could become members. In March 1959, the group of seven women borrowed Rs.80 from Changanlal Karamsi Parekh, a member of the servants of India society and a social worker. With this capital, they started making papads and selling them to a merchant known to them. Gradually the business grew and its membership increased. Within three months there were about 25 women making papads. Soon the women bought some equipment for the business.

The got considerable publicity through word-of–mouth and articles in vernacular newspapers. This publicity helped it to increase its membership. By the second year of its formation, 100 to 150 women had joined the group, and by the end of the third year more than 300 women were rolling papads. In 1962 the name Lijjat was chosen by the group for its products. It was recognized as a village industry by the Khadi and Village Industries Commission. The logo chosen read *'Symbol of Women Strength'*

SMGULP emphasized equality. All the members were considered equal and were referred to as sisters. All kinds of works were also given equal importance, no work was considered inferior or superior to any other. The women were also given the freedom to choose the work they liked best. Quality was also emphasized and supervisors constantly checked for quality and weight against set standards. Business was also done ethically. Care was taken to see that the products were priced reasonably, and whenever the cost of raw materials fell, the prices were also revised downwards. These revised prices were advertised in newspapers to ensure that the distributors did not overcharge. Products were marketed on an area wise basis. Each branch was individually responsible for marketing its products in the area allotted to it.

SMGULP's products were advertised in print and electronic media. The cooperative also sponsored some TV programmes and gave gift to winners of certain shows. SMGULP had managing committee consisting of 21 members. All the members were equal owners and shared profits equally at the end of the year. Mismanagement or loss due to negligence would lead to the dismissal of the concerned sanchalika. SMGULP took part in seven trade fairs and exhibitions held in various parts of India.

PROBLEMS AND CONSTRAINTS FACED BY WOMEN ENTREPRENEUR

1. Bank and other Financial Institutions do not consider Middle Class Women Entrepreneurs as "Serious" applicants for setting up their projects and they are hesitant to provide financial assistance to unmarried women or girls taking into consideration that who will return the loan either parents or in-laws. This humiliates unmarried women and they generally leave the idea to set up their ventures.
2. Attitude of Officers of Support System is not motivating and encouraging as they have the belief that setting up of business/industry is not the Women's cup of tea.
3. Financial Support System suffers from adhocism/ unpredictable delays.
4. Moving in and around the Market, is again a tough job for Middle Class Women Entrepreneurs in India Social system.
5. Women cannot get Sales Tax number (Regd.) without a male partner. This again humiliates prospective Women Entrepreneurs. This is male chauvinism at its worst and that too at the eve of the 21st Century.
6. The Security/Surety and collateral requirements of Banks and Financial Institutions specially frustrate unmarried women/girls. It is extremely difficult for girls and sometime other women also particularly those, coming from a lower socio-economic level to set up a modest sized unit as their own financial and other resources are barely inadequate to meet the promoter's contribution.

7. Man in the role of Father/Brother/Husband in general are not ready to accept entrepreneurship as career option for women in their homes, as it is unorganized and is full time activity.
8. Personal (family) reasons like : Women's more inclination towards family activity For married middle class women in India: 'Family is the priority'. For unmarried women: Marriage is the priority because of Indian social system.

SUGGESTIONS FOR PROMOTING WOMEN ENTREPRENEURSHIP

Right efforts on from all areas are required in the development of women entrepreneurs and their greater participation in the entrepreneurial activities. Following efforts can be taken into account for effective development of women entrepreneurs:

1. Consider women as specific target group for all developmental programmes.
2. Better educational facilities and schemes should be extended to women folk from government part.
3. Adequate training programme on management skills to be provided to women community.
4. Training and counselling on a large scale of existing women entrepreneurs to remove psychological causes like lack of self-confidence and fear of success.
5. Counselling through the aid of committed NGOs, psychologists, managerial experts and technical personnel should be provided to existing and emerging women entrepreneurs.
6. Continuous monitoring and improvement of training programmes.
7. Activities in which women are trained should focus on their marketability and profitability.
8. Making provision of marketing and sales assistance from government part.

9. To encourage more passive women entrepreneurs the Women training programme should be organised that taught to recognize her own psychological needs and express them.
10. Women's development corporations have to gain access to open-ended financing.

CONCLUSION

The women have proved themselves very successful entrepreneurs by engaging in one or two income generating ventures within the confines of their homes. All the women entrepreneurs discussed above in this chapter were able to overcome odds to create successful business ventures in their respective fields. They also an inspiration to a number of other women in India. Entrepreneurship among women, no doubt improves the wealth of the nation in general and of the family in particular. Women today are more willing to take up activities that were once considered the preserve of men, and have proved that they are second to no one with respect to contribution to the growth of the economy. Women entrepreneurship must be moulded properly with entrepreneurial traits and skills to meet the changes in trends, challenges global markets and also be competent enough to sustain and strive for excellence in the entrepreneurial arena.

REFERENCES

1. Educational Plus *(The Hindu)*.
2. BTL was set up in 1994, Major Content Provider to a Number of Prominent Channels Like Star Plus, Zee TV, Sony Entertainment Television.
3. ZEE Telefilms Limited is Promoted by Subhas Chandra, one of India's Leading Entrepreneurs.
4. *The Finance Express*, June-18 2001.
5. Kohli Vanita "Entertainment Value" *Business World* February 4, 2001 and December 2, 2002.
6. Management in Practice Edited By S.S. George.
7. *Business Today*, Special Issue September 26, 2004.

8. Dhameja SK (2002), Women Entrepreneurs: Opportunities, Performance, Problems, Deep Publications Pvt Ltd., New Delhi, p 11.

9. Rajendran N (2003), "Problems and Prospects of Women Entrepreneurs" SEDME, Vol. 30 No. 4 December.

10. Rao Padala Shanmukha (2007) "Enterpreneurship Development Among Women: A Case Study of Self Help Groups in Srikakulam District, Andhra Pradesh" *The ICFAI Journal* of Enterpreneurship Development, Vol.IV, No.1.

11. Sharma Sheetal (2006) " Educated Women, Powered, Women" *Yojana* Vol.50, No.1.

12. Shiralashetti A.S., and Hugar S S., " Problems and Prospects of Women Entrepreneurs In North Karnataka District: A Case Study" *The ICFAI Journal* of Entrepreneurship Development, Vol. IV, No. 2.

Index

❑❑❑